A Classic Double Envelopment

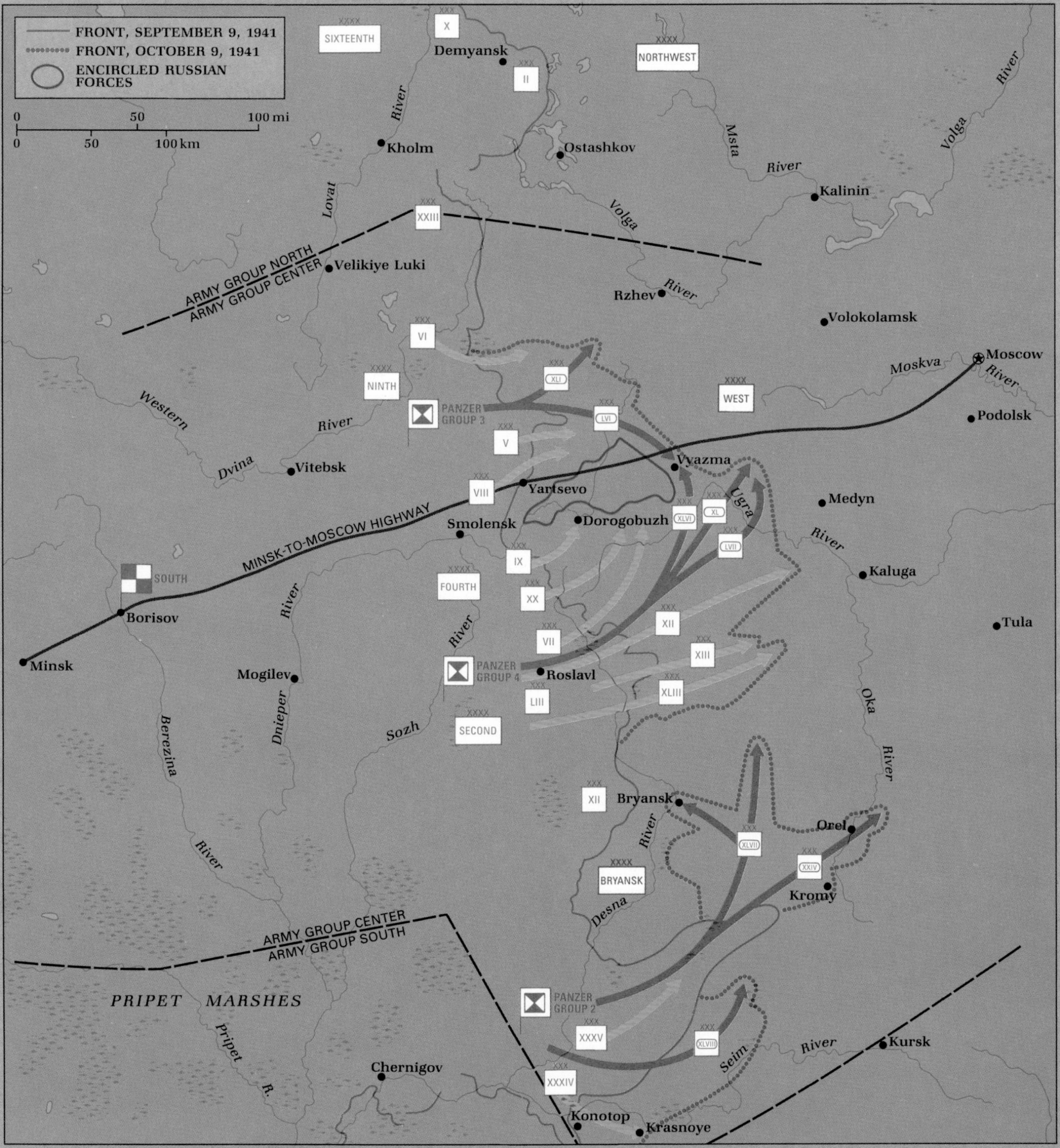

Legend:
- FRONT, SEPTEMBER 9, 1941
- FRONT, OCTOBER 9, 1941
- ENCIRCLED RUSSIAN FORCES

Scale: 0 — 50 — 100 mi / 0 — 50 — 100 km

Map labels (places and rivers):
SIXTEENTH · X · Demyansk · II · NORTHWEST · Kholm · Ostashkov · Kalinin · Lovat River · Msta River · Volga River · XXIII · Velikiye Luki · ARMY GROUP NORTH · ARMY GROUP CENTER · Rzhev · River · Volga River · Volokolamsk · VI · Moscow · Moskva River · Moscow River · NINTH · Western Dvina River · PANZER GROUP 3 · XLI · LVI · WEST · Podolsk · V · Vitebsk · VIII · Yartsevo · Vyazma · Medyn · XLVI · XL · Ugra River · Smolensk · Dorogobuzh · LVII · River · MINSK-TO-MOSCOW HIGHWAY · IX · Kaluga · SOUTH · FOURTH · XX · XII · Borisov · VII · XIII · Tula · Minsk · Mogilev · Dnieper River · PANZER GROUP 4 · Roslavl · XLIII · Berezina River · LIII · Oka River · Sozh River · SECOND · XII · Bryansk · Orel · Desna River · BRYANSK · Kromy · XLVII · XXIV · ARMY GROUP CENTER · ARMY GROUP SOUTH · PRIPET MARSHES · Pripet R. · PANZER GROUP 2 · XXXV · XLVIII · Seim River · Kursk · Chernigov · XXXIV · Konotop · Krasnoye

---

The quiet west of Moscow ended on September 30, 1941, when General Fedor von Bock's Army Group Center, headquartered at Borisov, launched Operation Typhoon. The attack surprised the Russians. Bock's armor (*dark red*)—Guderian's Panzer Group 2 in the south, Hoepner's Panzer Group 4 in the center, and Hoth's Panzer Group 3 in the north— sliced around the flanks and between two Red Army groups. In a week, they had encircled six Soviet armies west of Vyazma and were forcing three others into pockets southwest and northeast of Bryansk. The double envelopment netted 673,000 prisoners. But eliminating the pockets tied down most of Bock's infantry until late October, and many Soviet soldiers slipped out of the noose, escaping eastward to help defend the Mozhaisk Line in front of Moscow. Others disappeared into the forests to form partisan bands that would harass Bock's increasingly precarious supply lines.

This map is a corrected replacement for page 105 in The Third Reich volume *Barbarossa*, from which the type was inadvertently omitted.

War on the High Seas

By the Editors of Time-Life Books

Alexandria, Virginia

TIME
LIFE ®

Time-Life Books Inc.
is a wholly owned subsidiary of

The Time Inc. Book Company

President and Chief Executive Officer:
Kelso F. Sutton
President, Time Inc. Books Direct:
Christopher T. Linen

Time-Life Books Inc.

EDITOR: George Constable
Director of Design: Louis Klein
Director of Editorial Resources: Phyllis K. Wise
Director of Photography and Research:
John Conrad Weiser

PRESIDENT: John M. Fahey, Jr.
Senior Vice Presidents: Robert M. DeSena, Paul R.
Stewart, Curtis G. Viebranz, Joseph J. Ward
Vice Presidents: Stephen L. Bair, Bonita L.
Boezeman, Mary P. Donohoe, Stephen L.
Goldstein, Andrew P. Kaplan, Trevor Lunn,
Susan J. Maruyama, Robert H. Smith
New Product Development: Trevor Lunn,
Donia Ann Steele
Supervisor of Quality Control: James King

PUBLISHER: Joseph J. Ward

The Cover: Black smoke billows from the forward
turrets of the German battleship *Gneisenau* as its
gunners loose a salvo at British warships off the
coast of Norway on June 8, 1940. In this action, the
Gneisenau and its twin, the *Scharnhorst (foreground)*, sank the aircraft carrier *Glorious* and its
two destroyer escorts. Later they dispatched
twenty-two Allied ships during a single two-month
stretch.

This volume is one of a series that chronicles
the rise and eventual fall of Nazi Germany. Other
books in the series include:
The SS
Fists of Steel
Storming to Power
The New Order
The Reach for Empire
Lightning War
Wolf Packs
Conquest of the Balkans
Afrikakorps
The Center of the Web
Barbarossa

The Third Reich

SERIES DIRECTOR: Thomas H. Flaherty
Series Administrators: Jane Edwin,
Jane A. Martin
Editorial Staff for *War on the High Seas:*
Designer: Raymond Ripper
Picture Editor: Jane Jordan
Text Editors: Stephen G. Hyslop, John Newton,
Henry Woodhead
Writer: Stephanie A. Lewis
Researchers: Philip Brandt George, Paula
York-Soderlund (principals), Maggie Debelius
Assistant Designers: Bill McKenney,
Lorraine D. Rivard
Copy Coordinators: Anne Farr, Charles J. Hagner
Picture Coordinator: Jennifer Iker
Editorial Assistant: Jayne A. L. Dover

Special Contributors: Ronald H. Bailey,
George Daniels, Timothy Foote, Bayard Hooper,
Peter Pocock, Brian C. Pohanka, Curtis W.
Prendergast, David S. Thomson (text);
Martha-Lee Beckington, Ann-Louise Gates
(research); Michael Kalen Smith (index)

Editorial Operations
Production: Celia Beattie
Library: Louise D. Forstall

Computer Composition: Deborah G. Tait
(Manager), Monika D. Thayer, Janet Barnes
Syring, Lillian Daniels

Correspondents: Elisabeth Kraemer-Singh
(Bonn), Christine Hinze (London), Christina
Lieberman (New York), Maria Vincenza Aloisi
(Paris), Ann Natanson (Rome). Valuable
assistance was also provided by: Judy Aspinall,
Barbara Hicks (London); Elizabeth Brown,
Kathryne White (New York); Dag Christensen
(Oslo).

First printing. Printed in U.S.A.

Published simultaneously in Canada.
School and library distribution by Silver Burdett
Company, Morristown, New Jersey 07960.

TIME-LIFE is a trademark of Time Warner Inc.
U.S.A.

**Library of Congress Cataloging in
Publication Data**
War on the high seas / by the editors of
Time-Life Books.
    p.   cm. — (The Third Reich)
    Includes bibliographical references.
    ISBN 0-8094-6995-2
    ISBN 0-8094-6996-0 (lib. bdg.)
    1. World War, 1939-1945—Naval operations,
German.   2. Germany. Kriegsmarine—History—
World War, 1939-1945.   I. Time-Life Books.
II. Series.
D771.W284 1990   940.54'5943—dc20   90-10779

Other Publications:

TIME-LIFE LIBRARY OF CURIOUS AND UNUSUAL FACTS
AMERICAN COUNTRY
VOYAGE THROUGH THE UNIVERSE
THE TIME-LIFE GARDENER'S GUIDE
MYSTERIES OF THE UNKNOWN
TIME FRAME
FIX IT YOURSELF
FITNESS, HEALTH & NUTRITION
SUCCESSFUL PARENTING
HEALTHY HOME COOKING
UNDERSTANDING COMPUTERS
LIBRARY OF NATIONS
THE ENCHANTED WORLD
THE KODAK LIBRARY OF CREATIVE PHOTOGRAPHY
GREAT MEALS IN MINUTES
THE CIVIL WAR
PLANET EARTH
COLLECTOR'S LIBRARY OF THE CIVIL WAR
THE EPIC OF FLIGHT
THE GOOD COOK
WORLD WAR II
HOME REPAIR AND IMPROVEMENT
THE OLD WEST

For information on and a full description of any
of the Time-Life Books series listed above, please
call 1-800-621-7026 or write:
Reader Information
Time-Life Customer Service
P.O. Box C-32068
Richmond, Virginia 23261-2068

General Consultants

Robert O. Dulin, Jr., senior program manager at Basic Technology Corporation, and
William H. Garske, Jr., staff naval architect
at Gibbs and Cox, Incorporated, consulted
on the photographs and the cutaway of the
Bismarck. They are the coauthors of *Battleships,* Volumes 1 to 3. They advised the
Woods Hole Oceanographic Institution during its discovery of the *Bismarck* wreck.

Col. John R. Elting, USA (Ret.), former associate professor at West Point, has written
or edited twenty books, including *Swords
around a Throne, The Superstrategists,* and
American Army Life.

Charles S. Thomas is an associate professor at Georgia Southern University special-
izing in the study of twentieth-century Germany. He is a contributor to several works on
the history of the Third Reich and author of
The German Navy in the Nazi Era.

Charles V. P. von Luttichau is an associate
at the U.S. Army Center of Military History and
coauthor of *Command Decision* and *Great
Battles.* From 1937 to 1945, he served in the
German air force. After the war, he emigrated
to the United States and was a historian in the
Office of the Chief of Military History, Department of the Army, until he retired in 1986.

Contents

EINSATZ
DER DEUTSCHEN KRIEGSMARINE

The Shaky Debut of an Unfinished Fleet

The morning pace was leisurely aboard the German pocket battleship *Admiral Graf Spee*. On this tranquil Sunday, September 3, 1939, the vessel was ghosting through glassy mid-Atlantic waters 650 miles northwest of the Cape Verde Islands, trailed respectfully by its supply ship, the *Altmark*. As the tropical sun inched higher, the watch on deck sought the shade offered by the *Graf Spee*'s gun turrets and superstructure; a few off-duty sailors braved the heat to dangle fishing lines hopefully over the taffrail. On the bridge, Captain Hans Langsdorff drew contentedly, as usual, on a cigar.

The peaceful atmosphere belied the fact that the *Graf Spee* was on war alert—as were its sister ship, the *Deutschland*, patrolling far to the north off Greenland, and a total of twenty-two German U-boats prowling the western approaches to the British Isles. In mid-August, the German high command had ordered them all to sea, so that if war broke out they would not be trapped close to home. Then, on September 1, the Wehrmacht had launched an all-out assault on Poland, and ships of the German navy shelled the Polish coast. At first, most Germans thought that Great Britain and France would shrink from armed conflict and that the fighting would be contained. Indeed, Grand Admiral Erich Raeder, after conferring with Hitler, had assured his nervous subordinates that war with Britain was out of the question.

In any event, the *Graf Spee* was ready. Named in honor of an officer who had inflicted a stunning defeat on the British in the opening months of World War I, it was one of the most versatile warships of its time—a daunting combination of power, speed, and endurance. Sleek of silhouette with a towering fighting top, the *Graf Spee*'s welded hull was 609 feet long. The ship carried a crew of 1,150 and mounted six 11-inch guns with a range of fifteen miles, plus eight 5.9-inch and six 4.1-inch guns and eight torpedo tubes. It was powered by economical diesel engines that generated a top speed of twenty-six knots, and it had a remarkable range of 20,000 miles—enough to cruise for a month between fuelings. The *Graf Spee*, in short, was the quintessential high-seas raider, which was exactly what German strategy dictated that it be.

Warships parade beneath ominous clouds and a billowing battle ensign in this recruiting poster for the revived German navy. Such propaganda disguised the fact that the navy was ill equipped to face the gathering storm: When war erupted in 1939, Germany had only five new heavy warships.

Without warning, the *Graf Spee*'s Sunday morning calm was interrupted. The ship's radio shack, which routinely monitored British wireless traffic, had picked up an uncoded message: "11 a.m.: Commence hostilities at once against Germany." The intercept was rushed to Langsdorff on the bridge and was followed thirty-nine minutes later by a reciprocal message from *Seekriegsleitung*, or Supreme Naval Staff Headquarters, in Berlin: "Commence hostilities against England immediately." Langsdorff called the ship's company on deck to inform them that they were at war.

Mercifully, Langsdorff's men did not know how bleak the situation appeared to their superiors in Berlin. When Admiral Raeder announced to his aides that morning at Supreme Headquarters that Germany must now contend with the naval strength of both Britain and its ally France, the room fell silent. After a moment, Raeder adjourned the meeting and retired to

Rebels in navy uniforms brandish their weapons in Berlin during the upheaval that swept Germany as it confronted defeat in 1918. Dissidents in the traditionally conservative navy left their posts and agitated for radical change, but Admiral Raeder, stung by charges that the navy was treasonous, contended that such insurgents were outnumbered by civilian pretenders who "donned navy uniforms to gain acceptance to the revolutionary movement."

his office, where he penned a long and bitter memorandum. "Today, the war against England and France broke out," he wrote, "the war that, according to the Führer's previous assertions, we had no need to expect before about 1944." Trusting Hitler's word, Raeder had counted on five years' grace to complete his painstaking rehabilitation of the navy—a service that had been stifled, shamed, and all but destroyed at the close of the last war. Now a reluctant Raeder would have to pit the first proud symbols of the navy's renewal—including the *Graf Spee*—against potentially overwhelming opposition. As he noted darkly in his memo, his surface forces were "so inferior in number and strength to the British fleet that, even if they are used to the fullest, they can do no more than show that they know how to die gallantly."

Raeder's respect for British naval might was rooted in painful personal experience. As chief of staff to Vice-Admiral Franz von Hipper during World War I, he had looked on ruefully as the British, with the world's largest navy and firm command of the North Sea, kept the German High Seas Fleet bottled up in the Baltic Sea for the better part of four years. The one occasion when the entire fleet ventured out in force to meet the British resulted in the Battle of Jutland off the north coast of Denmark in 1916. The Germans fought skillfully, inflicting more punishment than they sustained. But the preponderance of the British Grand Fleet, which outnumbered the Germans three to two, forced the High Seas Fleet to retreat to port. Raeder, then a forty-year-old captain, emerged from the battle with a Knight's Cross for his performance under fire—and an indelible impression of the advantages conferred on Britain by the size of its fleet and its commanding position athwart Germany's sea lanes.

In the aftermath of Jutland, Raeder witnessed something far more disheartening: the demoralization of the penned-up German fleet. Dissatisfaction reached a peak in October of 1918, when the naval high command planned an expedition to cover the withdrawal of German troops from Flanders and rumors spread that the fleet was to be sacrificed merely to save the navy's honor. Mutinies erupted at Kiel, the navy's main base on the Baltic, and the operation had to be called off. The Kiel uprisings sparked a revolution in Germany that led to the abdication of Kaiser Wilhelm II and the birth of the Weimar Republic. Although dissident sailors played only a small part in this larger upheaval, the navy was branded as treasonous by conservatives opposed to the revolution—a charge that Raeder and his fellow loyalists among the service's elite never ceased to resent.

Ironically, the navy reclaimed some prestige in its hour of defeat through an act of sabotage. After the armistice in November, the Allies seized the bulk of the High Seas Fleet—about seventy vessels in all—and escorted the warships to the huge British naval base at Scapa Flow, in the Orkney Islands off the north coast of Scotland. There the ships lay at anchor for seven months while the victors pondered how to divide the spoils. Vice-Admiral Ludwig von Reuter, commandant of the captured fleet, had other ideas. At 10:20 on the morning of June 21, 1919, one week before the Versailles treaty was signed, he hoisted a signal flag that set in motion a secret plan to scuttle the fleet. Within an hour, two-thirds of the German ships lay on the bottom, the navy's honor perversely salvaged. In Raeder's view, it was "the one inspiring occurrence in that depressing spring of 1919."

Although the events at Scapa Flow offered some solace, the terms imposed on the navy at Versailles were devastating. Any warship built after 1913 had to be scrapped, and construction of submarines and military aircraft was forbidden. The treaty did allow the navy to retain in active service a limited number of older warships: six battleships and six cruisers built between 1899 and 1906, and twelve destroyers and twelve torpedo boats built between 1906 and 1913. But none of these ships could be replaced before it was twenty years old. And given Germany's postwar economic plight and the crushing reparations it was required to pay the Allies under the treaty, such replacements would be difficult if not impossible to finance.

Restrictions on personnel were equally Draconian. The navy, which had been second in size only to Great Britain's during the war, was limited to 15,000 men, including 1,500 officers. To twist the knife further, officers were required to sign up for twenty-five-year tours, and all other volunteers for twelve years. As it turned out, this provision proved no hindrance to recruiting: Germany's economic doldrums were such that, for years to come, scores of highly qualified candidates would apply for every opening. But the long terms hurt morale by limiting opportunities for promotion, and they prevented the navy from developing a large cadre of trained reservists who could be called up in time of war.

Raeder was among the seasoned officers who stayed on to restore the navy to respectability, serving as chief of staff to its new commandant, Vice-Admiral Adolf von Trotha. But Raeder's hopes that his battered service would soon regain the nation's full confidence were dashed in March 1920, when a former Reichstag representative named Wolfgang Kapp staged a coup against the fragile Weimar government with the help of an irregular brigade of right-wing navy veterans who marched into Berlin to support the putsch. Trotha unwittingly helped the rebels when, gulled into believing that the coup had succeeded, he pledged to support whatever new government emerged. In fact, the putsch lacked support and collapsed after

Ships of the German High Seas Fleet lie partly submerged in the shallows of Scapa Flow after their crews scuttled them in June 1919. Grand Admiral Erich Raeder wrote later that the defiant gesture "laid the foundation for the eventual reconstruction of the German fleet."

a few days. Trotha was forced to resign—and once again the navy's image was badly tarnished. Although Raeder was absolved of complicity in the plot by a board of review, he spent the next few years in posts that were less sensitive politically, compiling a history of cruiser warfare for the naval archives before becoming inspector of naval education in 1922.

The hiatus spared Raeder from involvement in a risky campaign by the German navy to rearm without alarming the Allied Armistice Control Commission or those political forces in Germany opposed to major rearmament. A few of the steps the navy took to increase its readiness were aboveboard: In 1921, work began on the first of the replacement vessels allowed by treaty, the light cruiser *Emden;* and over the next several years, a channel linking the navy base at Wilhelmshaven to the North Sea was

deepened to facilitate the passage of large warships. Yet the navy made its deadliest advances under cover. Researchers secretly designed a new magnetic mine—triggered by mere proximity to a ship's metal hull—that could be deployed from the air. To deliver such cargo, along with bombs and torpedoes, the navy developed various aircraft designs and later tried them out through a shadowy organization known as the Seaplane Testing Station for the United German Aviation Companies. The high command could not even dream of building an aircraft carrier in the 1920s, but engineers devised a catapult system to launch scout planes from warships. By far the most ambitious effort to skirt Versailles was the navy's bid to maintain its U-boat capability by channeling government funds to an obscure German engineering firm called IVS. Based in the Netherlands to divert suspicion, IVS contracted to design U-boats for foreign countries—including Turkey, Finland, and Spain—while on the side, the firm laid

A large crowd braves the rain at Wilhelmshaven on January 7, 1925, to witness the launching of the light cruiser *Emden*, the first replacement ship built for the German navy under the terms of the Versailles treaty. Austerity measures compelled the *Emden*'s designers to follow an obsolete, World War I plan.

As his weathered features
suggest, Erich Raeder (inset)
was a seasoned veteran when he
was named chief of the naval
command in 1928, having spent
thirty-four of his fifty-two years
in the navy. The son of a
schoolteacher, he had advanced
quickly and by 1912 was on
speaking terms with Kaiser
Wilhelm II, shown above in
white ducks during a Scandinavian tour; then-Commander
Raeder is on his left.

plans and accumulated parts for Germany's own future submarine fleet.

Funding schemes for the navy's covert projects were masterminded by Walter Lohmann, a captain on the staff of the high command. Lohmann's sleight of hand went undetected by the increasingly negligent Allied Armistice Control Commission. But in 1928, domestic critics of German rearmament got wind of Lohmann's unauthorized expenditures and demanded an accounting in the Reichstag. The investigation led to a house-cleaning: Lohmann resigned, as did his boss, Adolf Zenker, the navy's commander in chief. To fill the top spot, the government called on Raeder, who, again, was untainted by the scandal. Some feared that Raeder was too conservative and would meddle in politics. But his ambitions lay solely with the navy. So attached was he to the service and its starchy traditions that it was rumored he did not even own any civilian clothes. His navy pride

counted for little with his cabinet overseer, Defense Minister Wilhelm Groener, a retired army general who made it clear to Raeder that he was "no fleet enthusiast." But Raeder insisted before accepting the appointment that the navy remain independent of the army high command.

One of Raeder's assets in his new post was his courtly demeanor. (As a cadet, he had been so shocked by the language of his drill instructors that he had considered resigning from the service.) With characteristic tact, he mollified leading figures in the government and worked out an arrangement that allowed the most important of the covert projects—including mine-warfare research and the submarine program—to continue under a "sort of legality," as he put it. The compromise placed the projects on a secret budget that could be regulated by the government without alerting Germany's rivals. Meanwhile, Raeder forged ahead with the building of replacement ships in conformity with the Versailles treaty—a program that accelerated as the German economy improved. By the end of the decade, the navy would have a dozen new torpedo boats plus three 6,000-ton K-class cruisers—the *Königsberg, Karlsruhe,* and *Köln*—to join the *Emden.* These accomplishments were overshadowed, however, by a more ambitious and controversial undertaking: the plan to build pocket battleships.

The pocket-battleship concept was an ingenious response to a stringent clause in the Versailles treaty that limited future German warships to a displacement weight of a mere 10,000 tons. By contrast, the Washington Naval Treaties of 1921 and 1922 allowed the world's five leading sea powers—Great Britain, the United States, Japan, Italy, and France—to build battleships of up to 35,000 tons. Yet the Washington treaties offered the German navy a ray of hope by restricting the cruisers of the five powers to a 10,000-ton displacement and eight-inch guns; bigger weapons were allowed only if they could be considered experimental. The admirals in Berlin responded by drawing up plans for a 10,000-ton warship that would carry heavier guns than such cruisers while sacrificing nothing in the way of speed. The proposed vessel—the pocket battleship—would boast six 11-inch guns and eight 5.9-inchers. To keep its weight down, the ship would carry relatively light armor so that its eight diesel engines would give it twenty-six knots of speed—more than enough to elude rival battleships—and enormous range. On the drawing boards, at least, only Great Britain's three formidable battle cruisers—a class of vessel faster and as well armed as a conventional battleship but carrying lighter armor—would be able to outrun and outgun this new German threat.

When Raeder became chief of the naval high command in 1928, the project was nearing a test vote in the Reichstag, where critics of a costly arms buildup rallied around the cry, "Pocket battleship—or food for children?" To Raeder's relief, funding for the vessel was approved, though by the narrow margin of 255 votes to 203. It was a crucial victory, for the pocket battleship had become the linchpin of a new tactical plan. The navy was convinced that the traditional emphasis on massed fleets and squadrons was a thing of the past. Such large aggregations were easy to spot and left the navy with little flexibility. Instead, planners were emphasizing the need for task forces—smaller groupings of warships designed to fulfill specific missions. And what could be a better centerpiece for these task forces than the swift and powerful pocket battleship?

By the time the first such vessel, the *Deutschland*, was launched on May 19, 1931, the navy's morale was higher than it had been for a decade. In his christening speech, Chancellor Heinrich Brüning delivered a defiant message: "In this ceremony witnessed by the world, the German people are demonstrating that despite the shackles imposed upon them and all their economic problems, they have the strength to guard their peaceful existence and to defend their honor." Two more pocket battleships were on the way—the *Admiral Scheer* and *Admiral Graf Spee*. And over the next eighteen months, Raeder held to his expansive course even as political storm winds buffeted Germany. Before the Weimar Republic foundered early in 1933, he had won approval for a five-year plan that called for the construction of scores of vessels—including six full-size or pocket battleships and six cruisers; several squadrons of destroyers, torpedo boats, and minesweepers; and sixteen U-boats. The program, which flew in the face of the Versailles treaty, represented just the sort of bold thinking that Germany's aggressive new leader, Adolf Hitler, admired. And when Raeder first met with Hitler in February 1933, he pleased the Führer by announcing that the navy was "prepared to expand to any degree that might be necessary."

Hitler made it clear to Raeder in a later conference that the navy's mission was to bolster Germany against its rivals on the European continent, not to prepare for war with Britain. It was an assurance Hitler would repeat many times. Not only did he recognize the United Kingdom's dominance as a sea power; he hoped one day to reach an understanding with the British that would free him to pursue his territorial ambitions on the continent. For obvious reasons, Raeder was relieved to hear that there was no need to include the Royal Navy in his strategic plans. And having dealt with a succession of civilian leaders whose enthusiasm for defense matters rose and fell with the political tide, he was impressed by Hitler's firm commitment to naval rearmament, his grasp of detail, and his ability to cut to the heart of problems. Only gradually, and too late, did Raeder come to realize that Hitler was also hopelessly *landsinnig*—"land-minded"—and that he had little idea how to use the powerful navy they both wanted.

By March of 1935, German rearmament had proceeded to a point where Hitler felt free to repudiate the Versailles treaty. But he still had no desire to challenge the British. In a seemingly conciliatory move, he proposed a separate pact with London whereby Germany would limit its future naval tonnage to a level not to exceed 35 percent of Britain's. The proposal represented no real sacrifice on the part of the vastly inferior German navy: At the moment, the British surface fleet boasted 150 destroyers to Germany's 12, fifty-four cruisers to Germany's six, eight aircraft carriers to Germany's none, and twelve battleships and three battle cruisers to Germany's three pocket battleships. Yet the British were eager to pursue the proposal, for they faced a growing threat in Asian waters from Japan—which had already repudiated the Washington Naval Treaties—and they feared that the Royal Navy would be spread thin if Germany, too, embarked on an unrestricted naval buildup.

The agreement was signed on June 18, 1935, and was duly heralded by both sides. Speaking before the House of Lords, Admiral of the Fleet Earl Beatty said: "I am of the opinion that we owe thanks to the Germans. They came to us with outstretched hands and voluntarily proposed to accept a 35 to 100 ratio in fleet strength. If they had made different proposals, we would not have been able to stop them. That we do not have an armament race with at least one nation in the world is something for which we must be thankful." Raeder, for his part, welcomed the accord as confirmation that the navy could proceed with an orderly buildup, untroubled by the prospect of war with the world's greatest sea power. "As I look back now, this was a peak in our progress and in my own hopes," he wrote later. "I thought I had good reason to look to the future with confidence."

One result of the Anglo-German Naval Agreement was that Germany's U-boat development program at last emerged from the shadows. The Germans had yet to build a single U-boat for their own navy; however, submarines could be turned out at a much faster pace than battleships and cruisers, and the clandestine work by IVS in the Netherlands had given the Germans a running start. Less than four months after the signing of the Anglo-German agreement, the first twelve-boat submarine squadron put to sea for training exercises under Captain Karl Dönitz, a seasoned U-boat commander who had preyed on British vessels in the last war.

In addition to a potent submarine force, Admiral Raeder hoped to develop an air arm independent of any existing air force. He was convinced that such specialized tasks as long-range reconnaissance and tactical support for warships at sea required pilots who were schooled and commanded by the navy. Indeed, the navy already possessed a cadre of trained fliers when Hitler announced the existence of the Luftwaffe in 1935 and

The pocket battleship *Deutschland* towers above the spectators as President Paul von Hindenburg *(sword in hand)* and Chancellor Heinrich Brüning *(in civilian clothes)* review an honor guard at the launching ceremony in 1931. Workmen were eager to get the unfinished ship afloat; as Hindenburg addressed the crowd, someone inadvertently released the launching trigger and the *Deutschland* slid into the water.

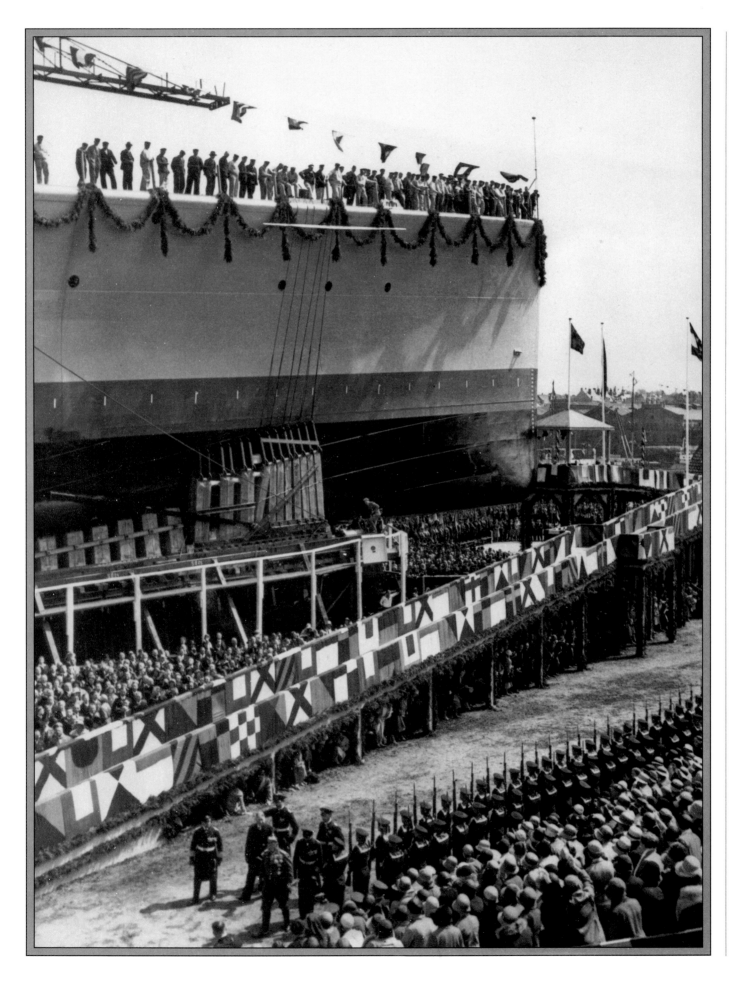

Denied its own air force, the German navy concentrated on perfecting aerial reconnaissance techniques. At left, a flying boat is hoisted aboard the tender *Ostmark*. The tender was equipped with a catapult *(below)* that propelled the plane down a runway for takeoff.

named his longtime aide, Hermann Göring, as its chief. Göring regarded German air power as his personal domain—he once boasted that "everything that flies belongs to me"—and he used his considerable influence to block Raeder's bid for a naval air force. The best deal that Raeder could get was Göring's agreement in 1936 to form a separate entity designated the Air Force Command (Sea); the Luftwaffe retained control over the selection of its planes and the training of its pilots, but the navy was granted future tactical control of the squadrons. Raeder turned over many of his existing pilots to this command in hopes of influencing its thinking. But the cards were stacked against him: By 1939, the navy was forced to sign a new pact with Göring that granted the Luftwaffe control of most air combat operations at sea, including aerial mining and attacks on enemy vessels and coastal bases. The navy had to content itself with jurisdiction over reconnaissance flights and close tactical support.

Raeder and his staff had little time to bemoan such setbacks. They were wrestling with fateful questions regarding the makeup and design of their expanding fleet. In the aftermath of the Anglo-German Naval Agreement, the buoyant high command ordered two big warships at a projected weight of 30,000 tons each: the *Scharnhorst* and the *Gneisenau*. These vessels would be comparable to enemy battle cruisers, although the Germans chose to classify them as battleships. The next German battleships on the drawing board—the *Bismarck* and the *Tirpitz*—would be true blockbust-

ers, exceeding 35,000 tons. But the navy first had to determine how to power its big ships. The diesel engines on the three pocket battleships of the *Deutschland* class had proved dependable and potent enough for vessels in the 10,000-ton range, but they might not be adequate for much larger loads. Recently, German engineers had come up with a promising alternative—a new type of turbine engine driven by superheated steam. The engine offered plenty of power, but questions remained as to its durability and efficiency. There was no time to test the two competing concepts in lengthy sea trials, so Raeder felt compelled to decide on the more powerful steam turbines and hope that the engineers could correct any flaws in the design. The decision would lead to trouble later on.

An even thornier issue remained—whether to expand the navy's roster of big vessels beyond the four battleships already projected or concentrate instead on building smaller, more maneuverable ships and submarines. The question became urgent in 1938, when Hitler's annexation of Austria soured relations between London and Berlin. In conversation, Hitler began referring to Britain and France as "those two odious enemies." And that August, he made it clear to an alarmed Raeder that Britain must indeed be considered a future adversary. Like it or not, the navy would have to face the bête noire of British sea power and set its construction priorities accordingly. The first such proposal to emerge at Supreme Headquarters was the work of Raeder's forty-three-year-old chief staff officer, Captain Hellmuth Heye, an outspoken critic of the traditional emphasis on big battleships. His plan was based on the assumption that Germany's fleet could never hope to outduel the Royal Navy and must instead outmaneuver it. "Britain's vulnerability lies in its maritime communications," Heye asserted. And that weakness could best be exploited through a swarming assault on merchant ships plying Britain's sea lanes—a campaign that called for a host of smaller vessels, with superior speed and range, rather than a small fleet of blockbusters.

The eight flag and staff officers who met with Heye to review his proposal were outraged. "Gentlemen," protested Vice-Admiral Günther Guse, "the plan of action that you have before you argues that we cannot successfully compete with Britain by means of battleships." To Guse, this was as good as conceding defeat. Heye's plan seemed to offer the German fleet no hope of breaking through a British blockade of its home ports—the very problem that had plagued it in the last war. As another admiral on the review committee insisted, "Only the heaviest ships could get the Atlantic striking force through." Heye replied that lighter ships with their greater maneuverability could thread the gaps in a blockade, but his critics were unconvinced. The review committee rejected Heye's arguments and submit-

Hitler greets an honor guard with a Nazi salute while Raeder (*left*) offers a conventional salute during the launching of the *Scharnhorst* at Wilhelmshaven on October 3, 1936.

ted to Raeder a revised, ten-year construction plan that included some huge vessels, including six monstrous type-H battleships of more than 56,000 tons. Concerned that Germany might stumble into war with Britain before such costly and time-consuming projects could be completed, Raeder revived the argument for a fleet of smaller, more elusive craft—including submarines—and presented it to Hitler as an alternative to the ten-year plan. In a report to the Führer, he summed up the two choices: *"Either* a force consisting mainly of submarines and pocket battleships that could be produced relatively soon and, though admittedly unbalanced, could in the event of war present a considerable threat to Britain's lifelines; *or* a force of great striking power, with capital ships of the highest class, that would take longer to produce but would threaten Britain's lifelines and engage the British Home Fleet with every prospect of success."

Given Hitler's fascination with prestige and power for its own sake, there could be little doubt as to his decision. The Führer had always been thrilled by big warships and loved to fill his sketchbooks with designs for battleships of gargantuan proportions. When he informed Raeder that he was opting for the more powerful alternative, the admiral felt compelled to warn once again that "if war breaks out in the next year or two, our fleet won't be ready." Hitler replied reassuringly, "For my political aims I shall not need the fleet before 1946."

In late January 1939, Hitler approved the ambitious buildup, known as Plan Z. In its particulars *(see table, page 20)*, the plan offered something for everyone, including the U-boat arm. But it was heavy with big-ticket items, including the six type-H behemoths and four aircraft carriers—all of them vessels that would take years to build and fit out. For Raeder, the months that followed were fraught with worry. On April 28, a few weeks after promoting Raeder to grand admiral, Hitler stunned him by abrogating the Anglo-German Naval Agreement. In an angry speech, he berated the British for siding with Poland in Germany's increasingly bitter arguments with its eastern neighbor. When Germany invaded Poland on September 1 and the Allies honored their commitment to the Poles two days later, all Hitler could do was admit stiffly to Raeder: "I wasn't able to avoid war with England after all."

The grandiose Plan Z was immediately abandoned, except for those surface ships that had been in the works before the list was approved and were nearing completion. From that point on, U-boats received top priority. New boats were ordered at the rate of twenty-nine per month—a level never achieved. It would be two years before Dönitz would have a fully effective undersea force at his command.

The navy's predicament could scarcely have been more alarming. The

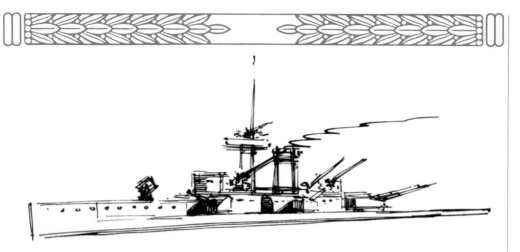

combined British and French forces now ranged against it numbered twenty-two battleships; the Reich could claim just two battleships and three pocket battleships. The Allies had seven aircraft carriers; Germany had one, the *Graf Zeppelin,* in the works, but more pressing military projects would prevent its completion. And Raeder's fleet was outnumbered ten to one in cruisers and nearly eight to one in destroyers and torpedo boats. The deficit in submarines appeared less worrisome: Germany now had 57 such vessels to the Allies' 135. But only twenty-two of the German boats were the oceangoing type; the rest were fit only for coastal service. Reflecting on the situation that September, Admiral Dönitz summed up the plight of his service: "The navy was like a torso without limbs. Seldom indeed has any branch of the armed forces of a country gone to war so poorly equipped."

Plan Z: Ship Construction Plans for 1938 to 1948

Type of vessel	Total to be built	Completed or almost completed by Sept. 1939
Pocket battleships	3	*Deutschland, Admiral Scheer, Admiral Graf Spee*
Battleships	10	*Gneisenau, Scharnhorst, Bismarck, Tirpitz*
Heavy cruisers	11	*Admiral Hipper, Blücher, Prinz Eugen, Seydlitz* (never used)
Light cruisers	22	*Nürnberg, Leipzig, Köln, Karlsruhe, Königsberg*
Aircraft carriers	4	*Graf Zeppelin* (never used)
U-boats	267	57
Scout cruisers	36	0
Destroyers	70	22
Torpedo boats	90	20
Training flotilla (old vessels)		*Schlesien* and *Schleswig-Holstein* (battleships) *Emden* (cruiser) *Horst Wessel* and *Gorch Fock* (sailing vessels)

The German navy's reluctant campaign on the high seas got off to a halting start. Raeder saw only one course: His surface fleet was no match for the opposition, so German warships would concentrate on raids and feints to divide and confuse the enemy. But even that plan was hobbled at first. Hitler was still convinced that the Allies would back down once they saw that his conquest of Poland was a fait accompli, and in the meantime he wanted to do nothing to rile them needlessly. Not long after Captain Langsdorff announced to the crew of the *Graf Spee* that they were at war, he received orders from Berlin instructing the *Graf Spee* and its sister ship, the *Deutschland,* to withdraw from operational areas until further notice.

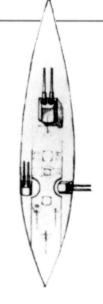

For the balance of the month, German attacks at sea were officially restricted to U-boat raids on warships and on merchant vessels that were armed or carrying war matériel—although one U-boat mistakenly torpedoed a passenger ship, the *Athenia*, on the first day of Anglo-German hostilities, claiming 118 lives. At the same time, the navy began laying its so-called West Wall—a series of defensive minefields along the North Sea that protected its bases from British incursions and offered a screen for German warships heading up the Norwegian coast toward the open ocean. In addition, the Germans laid offensive minefields along the coast of England. By month's end, the mines had claimed nine ships, and the U-boats another forty. The losses would have been worse in an unrestricted campaign, but that was little consolation to the Allies, who were unappeased by Hitler's half measures and showed no signs of yielding despite the collapse of Poland. Convinced now that there could be no turning back, Hitler told Raeder to unleash the surface fleet.

The admiral responded swiftly and adroitly, for the Allies had left him room to maneuver. Instead of concentrating on bottling up German warships in harbor or on providing escorts for merchant convoys, they formed so-called hunting groups to chase Germany's surface and undersea raiders "like cavalry divisions," as Winston Churchill put it. Such hunting expeditions used large numbers of ships to track down a few enemy vessels. Until the Allies changed their tactics, Raeder had an excellent chance to frustrate them. His plan called for the pocket battleships, which could outrun most pursuers, to target merchantmen with abandon; on September 30, the *Graf Spee* sank its first freighter in the South Atlantic, beginning a two-month spree. The big battleships, meanwhile, were to attack merchant shipping using hit-and-run tactics, thus drawing off as much enemy strength as possible while avoiding risky encounters. In early October, the *Gneisenau*, flagship of the German fleet, accompanied by the cruiser *Köln* and nine destroyers, slipped into the North Sea to harry the British Home Fleet. In November, the *Gneisenau* was joined by the *Scharnhorst*, which had recently overcome problems with its steam turbines, for a more ambitious foray. Raeder ordered the two battleships to defy enemy control of the vital passage between Iceland and the Faeroe Islands and make a feint into the North Atlantic to attract elements of the Home Fleet.

By the afternoon of November 23, the two German warships had threaded a course into the Norwegian Sea and were approaching the passage from the northeast, bucking heavy seas. Darkness was almost upon them when the fleet commander, Vice-Admiral Wilhelm Marschall, received word on his flag bridge that the *Scharnhorst* had spotted a large ship and was giving chase. He ordered the *Gneisenau* to follow in pursuit of the

quarry, which was laying a smoke screen and steaming at full speed toward the eastern horizon. At three minutes past five, the *Scharnhorst* opened fire with its eleven-inch batteries and, to its surprise, received a volley of six-inch shells in return. Eight minutes later, the *Gneisenau* added its weight to the barrage, and five minutes after that the battle was over, the steamer a blazing wreck whose fires were visible for miles. From its bridge a signal lamp flashed the desperate message "Please send boats."

The victim was the 16,700-ton *Rawalpindi*, a former P & O passenger liner recently converted to an armed merchant cruiser. Marschall had to assume that its captain had radioed his position and plight to friendly vessels; it was only a matter of time before elements of the British Home Fleet converged on the site. Nonetheless, the battleships briefly obeyed the rules of the Hague Convention governing naval conflict and flanked the stricken ship to try to pluck its lifeboats from the darkness and surging waves. They had pulled only twenty-seven survivors to safety when, at a quarter past seven, lookouts on both battleships spotted the outline of an approaching warship. It was the British cruiser *Newcastle*, which had picked up a message from the *Rawalpindi* incorrectly identifying its attacker as the *Deutschland*. The Royal Navy had been searching for the *Deutschland* since the outbreak of war, unaware that it had recently limped back to port for mechanical repairs. The *Newcastle* was not the only one to hear the signals. The Admiralty in London had intercepted them as well, and was already assembling a task force that would eventually include the battleships *Nelson* and *Rodney*, the battle cruiser *Hood* and its French counterpart, the *Dunkerque*, the aircraft carrier *Furious*, and more than thirty cruisers and destroyers. The latter were ordered to set up a picket line to prevent the Germans from fleeing eastward toward home.

At the moment, Admiral Marschall knew only that a single ship was shadowing him. He also knew that his standing orders were to avoid needless risk, and it was dangerous for a battleship to engage in night action against a vessel armed with torpedoes. Abandoning the effort to penetrate the North Atlantic, he ordered the *Gneisenau* and the *Scharnhorst* to steam northward at top speed and await further intelligence reports. Marschall learned nothing that night about the task force pursuing him, but he did discover from messages dispatched by disguised German weather ships that a major storm was brewing southwest of Greenland.

Marschall asked his staff meteorologist to predict when the storm would approach the Norwegian coast. After due study, the forecaster responded that at 7:00 a.m., November 26, the storm, packing gale-force winds, would be centered off the Norwegian port of Stadlandet. The *Gneisenau* and *Scharnhorst* withdrew almost to the Arctic Circle, and on November 25

German sailors prime a torpedo with compressed air during a 1937 exercise.

Marksmen in Training

With the increasing importance of squadrons of high-speed torpedo boats in Germany's expanding navy, training teams to fire the torpedoes became a vital element in preparing the Reich's sailors for war.

The standard torpedo, twenty-three feet long and weighing 1.5 tons, was an expensive piece of ordnance that the tightly budgeted German navy could not afford to waste. During exercises, the torpedo's detonator and explosives were removed, and the warhead was filled with water to replace the lost weight. Compressed air pushing out the water gave the torpedo its buoyancy at the end of its run.

The goal in practice was to come close to the target without hitting it and damaging the warhead. A smoke flare attached to the torpedo went off when the torpedo surfaced, enabling the boat crew to find and retrieve it.

After locating a spent torpedo by ▷
the smoke flare mounted in its
nose *(right)*, deck hands prepare
to hoist it back on board.

A dummy torpedo is launched
from tubes mounted on the deck
of a torpedo boat. The type-G7a
projectile shown here ran at
forty to forty-four knots to a
maximum range of eight miles.

An officer supervises crew
members using slings
and pulleys to lower the
recovered torpedo in place.
The torpedo will then be
reset and fired again.

began a furious dash southward under a low sky and through raging seas, hugging the Norwegian coast all the way. At midday on November 26, they broke unseen through the British cordon and reached Wilhelmshaven the following day—still undetected by the enemy but scarred by storm damage that would take months to repair. The British armada searched in vain for another three days before giving up in frustration.

In Berlin, relief at the safe return of the navy's biggest guns soon gave way to grumbling from those at headquarters who bridled at such evasive tactics. Shortly after the battleships reached Wilhelmshaven, Chief of Operations Kurt Fricke scrawled in the margin of Marschall's war diary, "Battleships are supposed to shoot, not lay smoke screens." And when Fricke learned that the two vessels had faced only a single enemy cruiser, he was beside himself. "They could have made a meal of her," he growled. "She was all alone." Yet Winston Churchill later offered a different assessment of the sortie. "We feared for our Atlantic convoys," he wrote, "and the situation called for the use of all available forces. But fortune was adverse." In short, Raeder's harassment had achieved its intended effect.

Raeder was hard-put to keep up the pressure, however. Of his five major warships, three—the *Gneisenau*, the *Scharnhorst*, and the *Deutschland*—were undergoing repairs, and a fourth, the *Admiral Scheer*, was being refitted. That left the *Graf Spee* to carry on alone. Undeterred, Captain Langsdorff was making the most of his opportunities. His primary hunting ground was the South Atlantic, but he was free to range north of the equator or to round either cape and prowl the Indian Ocean or the Pacific. With the supply ship *Altmark* nearby to siphon fuel and supplies from captured freighters, the *Graf Spee* could stay at sea indefinitely. It ran little danger of being spotted by radar or long-range aerial reconnaissance, since both of those techniques were in their infancy. Langsdorff's greatest concern was that one of his prey might radio its position to a nearby enemy warship before the *Graf Spee* could slip away.

After sinking the British freighter *Clement* off the eastern shoulder of Brazil on September 30, Langsdorff led the *Graf Spee* on a looping course across the South Atlantic. On October 7, the warship claimed two more victims, the *Ashlea* and the *Newton Beech*, followed by the *Huntsman* ten days later and the *Trevanion* five days after that. Langsdorff was using every trick in the sea raider's book. To confuse Allied intelligence in case he was spotted, he painted over the ship's name and transformed it into the *Admiral Scheer*; he sometimes flew British or French ensigns to lull his targets into a false sense of security until it was too late; he had the crew construct dummy funnels and turrets to alter the *Graf Spee*'s distinctive

A scout plane swoops in for a tricky open-sea landing during a hunting expedition early in the war. The crew of the *Gneisenau (far left)* will manipulate the ship's crane to pluck the aircraft from the sea.

silhouette; on one occasion he even transmitted a false signal to make any pursuers think the ship he was attacking was being torpedoed by a submarine. But in one vital respect, Langsdorff observed a strict and honorable code: By sending boarding parties ahead to seize the freighters and remove their crews before sinking them, he saved every man from every vessel, transferring the crews periodically to the *Altmark* while keeping the officers in relative comfort and dignity aboard the *Graf Spee.*

In late October, Langsdorff decided that it was time to throw the enemy off his scent. The *Graf Spee* turned southeast, rounded the Cape of Good Hope, and on November 15 sank the tanker *Africa Shell* near the coast of Mozambique. This time, Langsdorff let most of the crew escape to shore, knowing that they would spread the alarm. He hoped the Allies would scour the Indian Ocean looking for him while he doubled back on his tracks and returned to the South Atlantic. His caution was fully warranted, for the Allies had flung a wide net to snare the *Graf Spee*. Eight Anglo-French hunting groups were searching the waters off North and South America, the West Indies, France, Africa, and Ceylon. Twenty-two major warships were involved—a perfect example of the naval disruption Raeder wanted to achieve. When the *Graf Spee* attacked the 10,000-ton freighter *Doric Star* off West Africa on December 2, the task forces got their first real fix on the pocket battleship's whereabouts. Before the freighter went down, its radio operator repeatedly signaled its exact position—19°15' S, 5°5' E.

"That's a hell of a fellow," grumbled Langsdorff, who had instructed the doomed ship to maintain radio silence. "His damned signals will bring the whole British fleet about our ears." Nonetheless, Langsdorff took time to pick up the entire crew of the *Doric Star* before turning west. His plan was to make a final foray into the freighter-rich corridor off Buenos Aires, then head for home. The next day he paused to dispatch the 8,000-ton *Tairoa*. On December 6, he rendezvoused for the last time with the *Altmark* to top off his tanks and transfer prisoners to the supply ship, which now held more than 300 British crewmen under the stern eye of the *Altmark*'s notoriously Anglophobic captain, Heinrich Dau. The next day, the *Graf Spee* intercepted and sank another small steamer, the *Streonshalh*. Its tally now stood at nine ships of an aggregate 50,089 tons, still with no lives lost.

When word of the *Doric Star*'s distress signal was relayed to Commodore Henry Harwood, the four ships of his Hunting Force G were scattered along the east coast of South America; the nearest supporting group, the carrier *Ark Royal* and battleship *Renown*, were off Cape Town, South Africa. Harwood, a bluff, aggressive veteran, went to his charts to study the options open to his prey. They were numerous, but Harwood's instincts told him that the German warship would head for the mouth of the River Plate, the estuary where traffic from the nearby Uruguayan port of Montevideo and the Argentinian harbor of Buenos Aires—farther up the estuary—debouched into the Atlantic. He headed his flagship, the light cruiser *Ajax*, to a position 230 miles east of Montevideo. On the morning of December 10, the New Zealand light cruiser *Achilles* joined him. Two days later the heavy cruiser *Exeter* arrived to complete the task force; a fourth vessel, the heavy cruiser *Cumberland*, was refitting at the Falkland Islands 1,000 miles to the south. Harwood had drawn up his battle plan and signaled it to the *Exeter* and the *Achilles:* "Attack at once by day or night." If the engagement came by day, Harwood would try to counteract the enemy's superior firepower by dividing his force into two parts, with the *Ajax* and *Achilles* forming one unit and the larger *Exeter* the other. On December 12, Hunting Force G practiced its maneuvers and then secured to await the dawn.

When the sun edged above the horizon at 5:56 the next morning, a dozen pairs of binoculars on the three British ships swept the horizon in all directions, searching in vain for a sign of their prey. Reluctantly, Commodore Harwood ordered his men to stand down from action stations but to remain at full readiness. On the *Graf Spee*, meanwhile, the watches were going through the same anxious ritual, but with a different result. From the *Graf Spee*'s tall fighting top, the Germans sighted two tiny needles, and a moment later four more—the masts of three ships whose hulls were not yet visible. Alarm bells rang throughout the ship as the waking crew members hustled to action stations. At exactly 6:00 a.m., the pocket battleship was cleared for action. Soon the hulls of the distant ships rose high enough to be seen. One was identified as the *Exeter*. Captain Langsdorff assumed the other two must be destroyers protecting a convoy. In fact, the two unidentified vessels posed a more serious threat, but Langsdorff steamed confidently ahead and prepared to do battle.

The *Graf Spee* enjoyed several advantages over its opponents. With one broadside, it could unleash 4,140 pounds of shells, more than double what the *Exeter* could return and four times what the light cruisers could fire. Moreover, the British six- and eight-inch shells had far less chance of penetrating the pocket battleship's five-inch armor than the *Graf Spee*'s eleven-inch guns had of piercing the cruisers' thin sheaths. But the *Graf Spee*'s biggest edge was one that the overconfident Langsdorff failed to take advantage of—its longer reach. Had he chosen to do so, Langsdorff could have stayed outside the cruisers' range all day and pounded away with impunity. Instead, the ships continued to bear down on one another at a combined speed of more than forty knots. Fully alert now to the threat, the British ran up their battle ensigns.

At 6:18 a.m., the *Graf Spee* launched its first salvos from a distance of more than eleven miles, near the limit of the cruisers' ability to respond. To Commodore Harwood's surprise, the German ship continued to close in, and at 6:22 a.m. the British began returning fire. For the next seventy-five minutes, the four vessels blasted away at brain-numbing, earsplitting twenty-second intervals. Harwood divided his force as planned, flanking his enemy to the north with the *Ajax* and the *Achilles*, while the *Exeter* moved to the south. At first Langsdorff split his fire between the two forces,

but soon he decided to concentrate all his batteries on his larger foe. The results were devastating: Within minutes, a shell crashed through the forward deck of the *Exeter* and exploded; then another hit the bridge, killing or badly wounding everyone there except the captain, F. S. Bell. Its internal communications cut, the *Exeter* was out of control, surging in giant figure eights at thirty knots while explosives continued to rain down. One gun turret was knocked out, a major fire broke out amidships, and another shell holed the waterline. Captain Bell groped through smoke and chaos to the emergency conning station in the stern. There he set up a chain of men to relay his voice commands below to other crew members, who tried frantically to manhandle the rudder back under control. The stern guns were still firing, but the ship was down at the bow and listing at least ten degrees to starboard with tons of water flooding in. Bell decided that his only recourse was to ram the *Graf Spee* and take it down with him. Then, just after half past seven, the shelling stopped.

The reprieve, which seemed nothing short of a miracle to the crew of the *Exeter,* was in fact the result of resourceful work by its two smaller partners. Seeing the terrible pounding the *Exeter* was taking, the *Ajax* and the *Achilles* had formed up to the north in an attempt to draw the tormentor off, but from a prudent range their salvos had no visible effect. "We've got to draw his fire," shouted Harwood aboard the *Ajax.* "At this range we might as well bombard the beast with snowballs." Moving brashly to point-blank range, the two light cruisers adopted destroyer tactics, firing torpedoes and steering toward the *Graf Spee*'s previous shell splashes in the hope of dodging the next ones. The evasive maneuver was a success but not a complete one. One eleven-inch shell hit the *Ajax,* knocking out two turrets.

The ferocity of the British attack startled Langsdorff. The galley of the *Graf Spee* had been wrecked and the ship's fresh-water supply fouled, a shell hole six feet by three feet gaped above the waterline, several small guns had been knocked out, and there was additional damage and fire the length and breadth of the vessel. Langsdorff had suffered a concussion and wounds to his face and arm, thirty-seven of his officers and men were dead, and another fifty-seven badly injured. To be sure, the ship's engines and heaviest guns were intact. But Langsdorff, having first underestimated the opposition, was now inclined to fear the worst. "The *Ajax* and her sister ship came at me like destroyers," he explained later. "I thought they were trying to drive me into the guns of bigger ships." Daunted, the German skipper broke off the action and headed for Montevideo.

The *Ajax* and the *Achilles* shadowed the pocket battleship at a respectful distance. Captain Bell, meanwhile, had regained control of the *Exeter.* He reported to Harwood that his ship was no longer taking on water and

In pictures taken from the pocket battleship *Admiral Graf Spee,* an explosion *(top)* rends the British freighter *Ashlea* on October 7, 1939, shortly after a boarding party from the *Graf Spee* seized the vessel. The boarders set charges on the freighter and returned by launch with its crew as the *Ashlea* foundered *(bottom).*

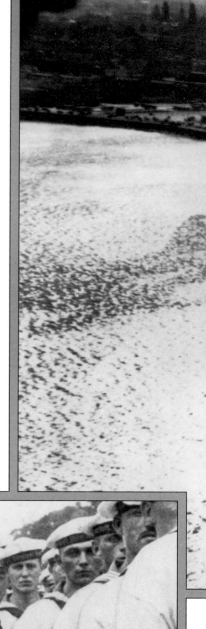

remained seaworthy. Harwood ordered the *Exeter* to the Falklands for repairs, trusting that the heavy cruiser *Cumberland* had heeded his signals and was sailing north from the Falklands to assist. The *Exeter* steamed away, hugging the shoreline in case Bell was forced to beach the ship. That afternoon, he buried four officers and forty-seven of his men at sea.

Once in port, Langsdorff had to face an even more bewildering contest, a five-day diplomatic dispute over the fate of his ship played out by representatives of Uruguay, Argentina, Britain, France, and Germany—while in Berlin, Raeder and Hitler waited on tenterhooks, unable to help. The *Graf Spee* had entered neutral waters, and under the Hague Convention it could remain only long enough to be rendered seaworthy again, not to rearm for battle. When his ship dropped anchor just before midnight on December 13, the exhausted captain had been on the bridge for more than eighteen hours. He was still wearing only pajamas, a sweater, and seaboots under his bridge coat. First he had to face Uruguayan port inspectors. Then, at half past three in the morning—his facial wounds dressed but still oozing blood and one arm in a sling beneath his coat—he went ashore to confer with the German ambassador and Uruguay's foreign minister. Langsdorff was told only that he would be accorded every courtesy under

Above, the *Graf Spee* finds temporary refuge in the inner harbor at Montevideo, Uruguay, on December 14, 1939, one day after its shootout with British cruisers. While mechanics began work on the ship, Captain Hans Langsdorff went ashore in dress whites to bury his dead *(left)*.

international law and that an inspection team would come aboard in the morning to assess the damage.

The two British cruisers waited offshore, low on fuel and ammunition and still very much alone. They were in no position to block the broad River Plate—more than 100 miles wide at its mouth. Harwood knew that if the German ship decided to break out, its chances of slipping past them were excellent. And if it came to another battle, he put the chances of either the *Ajax* or the *Achilles* surviving at no more than 30 percent. Nonetheless, he maneuvered as close as he dared to the three-mile limit from shore mandated by international law, hoping to cover any attempt at escape.

Langsdorff saw the *Graf Spee*'s predicament quite differently. Convinced that his ship needed major work before attempting a winter dash across the North Atlantic, he requested two weeks in port for repairs. The Uruguayans inspected the damage and promised an answer soon. In the meantime, Langsdorff began repair work, freed his sixty-one captive mer-

Explosions shatter the *Graf Spee* at twilight on December 17 after Captain Langsdorff—faced with internment—ordered the ship scuttled. More than 500,000 people watched from shore as explosives planted by the crew ignited what one witness described as a "witch's cauldron blazing away in the sea."

chant officers, transferred fifty of his most seriously wounded crew members to hospitals, and organized a funeral ashore for his dead. Even the newly released British officers sent a delegation to the ceremony. As the dead were lowered to their graves, Langsdorff offered them a traditional military salute, in conspicuous contrast to the stiff-armed Nazi salute raised by some of his compatriots. After the ceremony, he learned that Uruguay, under pressure from the Allies, would allow the the *Graf Spee* only seventy-two hours in port. To Langsdorff, it seemed a death sentence.

By now the British were sending signals that they hoped would be intercepted, describing the convergence of a formidable task force at the mouth of the Plate to bottle up the *Graf Spee.* These false reports so impressed some of Langsdorff's officers that they interpreted ambiguous sightings of vessels in the distance as confirmation that the phantom task force was already in control of the estuary. In light of these claims, Langsdorff reviewed his options. He could try to smash through what he believed to be overwhelming British opposition, an effort that he felt sure would end in the destruction of the *Graf Spee* and its crew. He could make a run up the Plate to Buenos Aires, where the sympathetic Argentines might offer sanctuary; but the estuary was relatively shallow there, and mud might easily be sucked in through the ship's cooling-water intakes at the bottom of the hull, causing the engines to seize up before the *Graf Spee* reached safe harbor. He could request internment in Uruguay, but Berlin quickly vetoed that option, fearing that the Uruguayans were too friendly with the Allies and might one day hand the interned ship over to them. Or, he could scuttle the *Graf Spee*. As the three-day term allowed for repairs neared its hour of expiration—8:00 p.m. on December 17—Langsdorff concluded that the last option was the only viable one.

All that Sunday aboard the *Ajax,* the vigilant Harwood received reports of unusually brisk activity in the harbor; men were being ferried from the *Graf Spee,* and huge crowds were flowing toward the quays and breakwaters that bordered the shore. Harwood, who had just learned by radio from London that he had been promoted to rear admiral, assumed that his adversary was preparing to come out with a skeleton crew of volunteers and make a fight of it—one that could be fatal to all of them. He ordered his ships to close up to the three-mile limit on first-alert status.

Shortly after five that afternoon, the *Graf Spee* hoisted a large Nazi ensign, weighed anchor, and proceeded slowly out to sea followed by the German merchant vessel *Tacoma.* As the great ship approached the boundary of international waters, it slowed, maneuvered to shallow water at the edge of the channel, and dropped anchor. In the gathering darkness the waiting cruisers saw a huge explosion, then another, and a third. Scuttling teams

had positioned torpedoes over each ammunition magazine, and soon the entire *Graf Spee* was ablaze and shuddering with massive eruptions of smoke and flame. Langsdorff and his men watched from the deck of the *Tacoma* as cheers of relief and exultation echoed from the British cruisers.

That night, Langsdorff and his men were transported upriver for internment in Buenos Aires. There, on the evening of December 19, Langsdorff spoke to his crew for the last time. "A few days ago, it was your sad duty to pay the last honors to your dead comrades," he remarked in closing. "Perhaps you will be called on to undertake a similar task in the future." Langsdorff continued in that cryptic vein after the speech, when newspaper correspondents approached him for an interview. "There's no story tonight," he replied courteously, "but there will probably be a big one for you in the morning."

Returning to his quarters, Langsdorff wrote a lengthy note to the German ambassador, who had tried to help in the negotiations for his ship. "I decided from the beginning to bear the consequences involved in this decision," he explained. "For a captain with a sense of honor, it goes without saying that his personal fate cannot be separated from that of his ship. I can now only prove by my death that the fighting services of the Third Reich are ready to die for the honor of the flag." Then he unrolled an ensign of the old German Imperial Navy, draped it around his shoulders, and put a bullet through his head.

The scuttling of the *Graf Spee* infuriated Hitler, who publicly defended Langsdorff's decision but privately made it clear to Raeder that German ships must never go down without a fight. Accordingly, Raeder reminded his commanders that once a navy vessel was decisively engaged with the enemy, it must battle to "the last shell with the full commitment of its crew until it is victorious or until it goes under with banners flying." In effect, Hitler had thrown down a challenge, and the navy would soon have ample opportunity to respond. ✠

At right, above, Captain Langs-dorff *(arm extended)* maintains a cheerful front with his men, masking his resolve to end his life after the loss of the *Graf Spee*. Langsdorff delayed his suicide long enough to accompany his men by tug to Buenos Aires *(inset)*, where they were interned. After his death, members of the crew bore his body to the grave *(right)*; among the mourners was the newly freed captain of the *Ashlea*, an earlier victim of the *Graf Spee*.

A Modern Monster of the Seas

The ultimate exemplar of the revitalized German navy was the battleship *Bismarck*, which with its sister ship, the *Tirpitz*, was the heaviest warship ever commissioned by a European nation. Four years of planning and four more of construction at Hamburg's Blohm & Voss shipyard came impressively to fruition on August 24, 1940, when the mighty vessel, its size matched by its state-of-the-art military technology, was commissioned into the navy.

The *Bismarck* was unusually broad beamed (118 feet) in proportion to its length (792 feet). Compensating for this characteristic, which could have severely limited the ship's speed, was a steam-turbine, single-reduction-gear propulsion plant capable of generating 136,200 horsepower. The *Bismarck*, with a maximum speed of almost thirty knots, was one of the fastest battleships afloat. Its hefty beam had the advantage of providing a stable firing platform for an imposing array of armaments.

The ship's four main turrets, two fore and two aft, (named Anton, Bruno, Caesar, and Dora) each housed twin fifteen-inch guns with a maximum range of more than twenty miles. Three armored control stations directed their fire, using sophisticated stereoscopic range finders and radar mounted on rotating cupolas. Secondary armament consisted of three twin turrets of 5.9-inch guns mounted on either side of the ship and sixteen 4.1-inch antiaircraft guns supported by an additional thirty-two smaller guns.

The *Bismarck*'s designers ensured that the battleship could take punishment as well as deliver it. Armor plating accounted for more than one-third of the ship's battle-load displacement of 50,129 tons, with special emphasis on underwater protection against mines, torpedoes, and near-miss bomb explosions.

As shown in the cutaway on the following pages, the *Bismarck* was a virtually self-contained community. In addition to quarters for the 2,065-person crew and support staff, below-deck facilities included hangars for four Arado floatplanes, an infirmary, a shoe-repair shop, and a laundry. Refrigerated food lockers held 300 sides of beef and 500 whole pigs.

It was the ship's overwhelming aura of invulnerability, however, that most impressed observers. "She was a technological triumph," a young officer assigned to the *Bismarck* recalled. "At first sight, I felt sure that she would rise to any challenge, and that it would be a long time before she met her match."

The intimidating scale of the *Bismarck* is evident in this painting, which depicts the battleship beginning a turn to port after sailing from Norway on May 21, 1941.

Inside the Mighty Bismarck

The main armor belt is outlined in red.

1. Officers' staterooms
2. Clothing storeroom
3. Trimming tank
4. Warrant officers' baggage room
5. Rudders
6. Steering gear room
7. Warrant officers' mess
8. Steering motor room
9. Propellers
10. Master chief petty officer's living quarters
11. Hand steering room
12. Propeller shaft
13. Fuel tanks
14. Warrant officers' living quarters and mess

15. Chief petty officers' living quarters and mess
16. 15-inch cartridge magazines
17. Pair of 15-inch guns
18. Turret Dora
19. 15-inch turret machinery platform
20. Ammunition hoist
21. 15-inch shell rooms
22. Pair of 15-inch guns
23. Turret Caesar
24. 5.9-inch fire-control director
25. 37-mm gun (16)
26. 20-mm gun (16)
27. Admiral's and captain's staterooms
28. Air intake
29. Center engine room
30. Aft fire-control station

31. Aft 15-inch range finder
32. Twin 4.1-inch guns (16)
33. Wardroom
34. 4.1-inch cartridge magazines
35. Searchlight control station
36. Arado 196 scout plane
37. Twin 5.9-inch guns (12)
38. Mainmast
39. Captain's motor launch
40. Turbine room
41. Machine shop
42. Catapult
43. Aircraft positioning crane
44. Searchlight
45. Funnel
46. Uptakes from boiler
47. Boiler room
48. Air-intake louvers

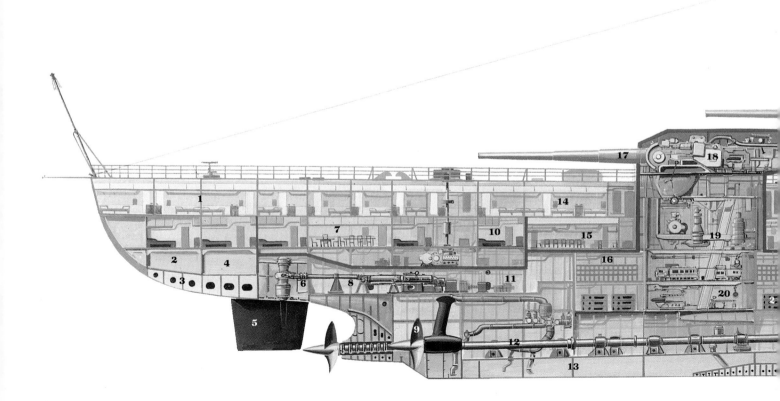

The main armor belt is outlined in red.

49. Foremast
50. Foretop main battery range finder
51. Foretop fire control
52. Searchlight
53. Admiral's bridge
54. Range finders with radar
55. Chart house
56. Auxiliary machinery room
57. Central damage-control station
58. Conning tower
59. Sick bay
60. Antiaircraft-gun repair shop

61. Forward gunnery computation room
62. Refrigeration machinery room
63. Turret Bruno
64. 15-inch gun at 30° maximum elevation
65. Main battle-dressing station
66. Armored barbette cylinder
67. Turret Anton
68. Crew living and mess spaces
69. Anchor windlass machinery room
70. Boatswain's storeroom
71. Fuel-transfer pumps and manifolds
72. Lumber storeroom

73. Windlass
74. Chain lockers
75. Fuel tanks
76. Canvas storerooms
77. Cordage storeroom
78. Starboard anchor
79. Spare bow anchor
80. Main deck
81. Battery deck
82. 'Tween deck
83. Upper platform deck
84. Middle platform deck
85. Lower platform deck
86. Paravane tube

TWO

Campaigns of Stealth and Deception

Embarking for the invasion of Norway, German mountain troops file aboard the heavy cruiser *Admiral Hipper* in the North Sea port of Cuxhaven as scores of the ship's crewmen watch on April 6, 1940. To keep the preparations secret, Cuxhaven's Weser River was closed to all traffic while the embarkations took place.

efore noon on October 17, 1939, six weeks after the beginning of the war, a squadron of half a dozen German destroyers sailed from the North Sea port of Wilhelmshaven, bound for the enemy coast. To deceive any British reconnaissance planes that might be snooping overhead, the ships steered a northward course. Then, when dusk fell and the danger of aerial detection diminished, they veered sharply westward and headed for the mouth of the Humber River on the east coast of England, some 250 miles from their starting point. Steaming at their top speed of thirty-eight knots, they slipped through the night into the waters between the Humber estuary and the Withernsee Lighthouse, the shipping lane to the bustling port of Hull and one of the busiest mercantile channels in the world. Here, shortly after midnight, the crews quickly and stealthily set to work in the inky darkness without a single light to betray their presence.

While one of the destroyers, the *Wilhelm Heidkamp*, stood sentinel, the five others disgorged their lethal cargoes. On the afterdeck of each vessel, gangs of seamen hefted mines onto long sets of rollers. The mines were big, black, and menacing, as tall as the men who wrestled with them. As the mines rumbled down the slight incline, they gained momentum and then, at the stern, splashed one by one into the black water. When each destroyer exhausted its supply, it set a swift course for home. The mission was carried out so quietly and efficiently that the British had no idea unwelcome visitors had paid a call. Four days later, however, a thunderous explosion told them something was amiss. On that day, October 22, the newly sown field of 300 mines claimed its first victim, a 1,692-ton merchant steamer. Eventually, a total of seven ships amounting to nearly 26,000 tons ran afoul of the mines laid by the single squadron of destroyers in one night.

That mission was the first of many successes in an extensive mine-laying campaign along the British coast undertaken to disrupt British commerce. Although it lacked the drama of big ships clashing on the high seas, the silent campaign nevertheless caused the Royal Navy a great deal of trouble and worry. The mining operations were soon followed by other ventures that involved every kind of surface vessel, from destroyer to battleship, in

A Worldwide Reach for Dominance

Ships of the Kriegsmarine began the war by sowing minefields in the estuaries of Britain's east coast (*inset, far right*), then sortied to Scandinavian ports during the seaborne invasion of Norway and Denmark (*inset, below*). German capital ships slipped through the British naval cordon into the North Atlantic to attack Allied convoys, often withdrawing to the German-occupied ports of France. Heavily armed raiders disguised as merchant vessels stalked the east coast of South America and west coast of Africa, and roamed as far as the Indian Ocean and South Pacific in search of Allied prey.

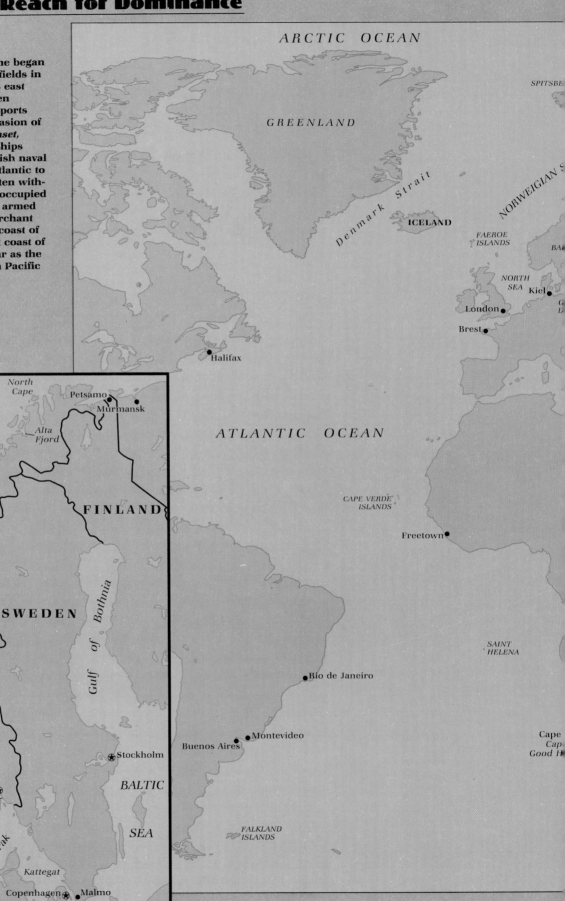

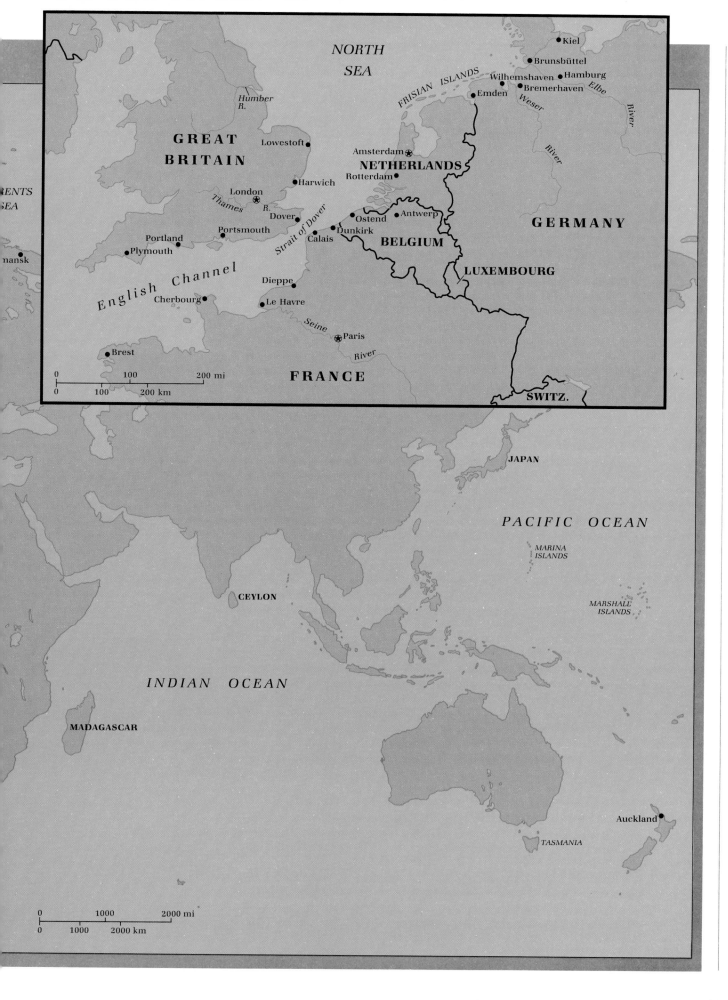

every sort of campaign, from commerce raiding to the invasion of Norway. For about a year and a half, Admiral Raeder's small fleet enjoyed a string of victories; it was a time when daring tactics paid off again and again.

The key to the early campaign in British coastal waters was a new and secret magnetic mine. Unlike conventional, contact mines, which detonated when a ship struck one of their protruding spikes, the new devices exploded in response to the magnetic fields generated when steel-hulled ships passed over them. Magnetic mines worked best in shallow water and were therefore ideal for the English estuaries, which seldom exceeded a depth of ninety feet. The devices were also immune to conventional minesweeping methods. To destroy contact mines, a minesweeper deployed a sawlike device that cut the cables mooring the submerged mines to their anchors. The mines then floated to the surface, where they could be exploded by gunfire. Magnetic mines, which rested on the bottom, were beyond the reach of minesweepers.

The first magnetic mines were laid by German submarines. Gliding submerged into British harbors and estuaries, the U-boats launched the mines through their torpedo tubes and slipped away undetected. German destroyers, meanwhile, were sowing huge fields of the more plentiful contact mines along their home coasts as a defensive measure against British naval raids. The so-called West Wall that they created stretched 150 miles from the Dutch coast up into the Skagerrak, the arm of the North Sea between Denmark and Norway.

The German fleet of twenty-two destroyers soon took over the task of laying mines in British waters. A destroyer could carry ten times as many mines as a U-boat, and its high speed enabled it to dart into a British estuary at nightfall, drop its load, and be safely headed for home before dawn. Yet destroyers packed powerful enough weaponry—four torpedo tubes and five 5-inch guns—to fight back if challenged by British ships.

In November, as the nights grew longer and extended the protective cloak of darkness, the destroyers escalated their mine-laying activities. The main target was the wide mouth of the Thames River. Laced with channels and sandbanks, dotted with lightships and buoys and alive with cargo vessels heading to and from London's docks, the Thames estuary was hair-raising territory for a German destroyer.

Yet the rewards seemed well worth the risk. On the night of November 12, the *Hermann Künne* and two other destroyers sowed 288 magnetic mines in the mouth of the Thames. As a result, a British destroyer, the *Blanche*, was sunk, and traffic in two of the estuary's three deepwater channels was disrupted. Returning on the night of November 17, the *Hermann Künne* escorted two other destroyers as they laid 180 mines in

the third channel. The next night, a trio of destroyers revisited the heavily traveled Humber River farther north, laying mines that soon sank seven merchant ships. A few nights later, a minefield off Harwich on the northern shore of the Thames estuary claimed another British destroyer, the *Gipsy*.

The British, confronted with mounting losses so close to home, were dumbfounded. Under the very noses of the Home Fleet, mines were doing more damage to shipping than the vaunted German U-boats stalking the Atlantic. During the month of November alone, mines sown by German destroyers sank twenty-three ships. The British had experimented with magnetic mines, which they called ground mines, and they finally recognized that these devices were causing most of the damage. But they remained confused about the source of the mines. Since they had detected no intruders on the surface, they incorrectly surmised that U-boats must be laying the mines and therefore took no countermeasures against the German destroyers that were mainly responsible. "A new and formidable danger threatened our life," Winston Churchill later wrote. "The terrible damage that could be done by large ground mines had not been fully realized." Hitler, for his part, was delighted when Raeder told him of the exploits of the hitherto unheralded destroyers, even boasting in a speech that the German navy "has swept the North Sea clear of the British!"

The German navy, of course, had achieved nothing of the kind. The North Sea still swarmed with British submarines and surface ships. Raeder and his staff officers deemed them such a menace, in fact, that they routinely detailed cruisers to stand by in the North Sea off the entrance to the Skagerrak to escort the destroyers home after their mine-laying missions. This was the reverse of the usual practice, in which destroyers escorted cruisers and other larger ships, and it brought dire consequences.

The trouble came on the morning of December 13 when three German cruisers—the *Leipzig*, the *Nürnberg*, and the *Köln*—were on patrol in the entrance of the Skagerrak, waiting for five destroyers that had been sowing mines off the port of Newcastle, a major assembly point for British convoys. The destroyers' sortie would prove to be highly effective: The mines laid that night would sink no fewer than eleven ships. As noon approached, however, the destroyers were still some 130 miles west of the rendezvous area. They had been delayed first by an engine fire, then by an attack by German aircraft that had mistaken the ships for British vessels.

The crewmen of the waiting cruisers had reason to be anxious. As a rule they brought their own escorts, usually destroyers and speedy torpedo boats that were effective against submarines. But this time no torpedo boats had been available, and all the destroyers not engaged in laying mines were under refit or repair. The cruisers were alone, and exposed.

About half past eleven, the cruisers were suddenly attacked by the British submarine *Salmon*, which had been enjoying an unusually eventful patrol. Nine days earlier, it had accomplished the rare feat of sinking another submarine, the U-36, with a torpedo. The previous day, it had been in position to stop the 51,000-ton passenger liner *Bremen* before a Dornier 18 flying boat escorting the giant German ship forced the *Salmon* to crash-dive. Now, in the same waters, the British submarine sighted the three German cruisers, took aim, and fired a succession of six torpedoes.

One of them slammed into the *Leipzig* amidships and blew apart its port boiler rooms. The two other cruisers turned hard, attempting to present their bows as smaller targets, but soon the *Nürnberg* was also hit, a torpedo smashing into its starboard bow. Three of the mine-laying destroyers at last arrived that afternoon to shepherd the two crippled cruisers back to port, and on the next day several torpedo boats met the *Leipzig* to assist in the escort. Even then, the German ships were not safe. As they neared the mouth of the Elbe River, the British submarine *Ursula*, operating in perilously shallow water, scored a hit on one of the *Leipzig*'s escorting torpedo boats, which sank quickly with few survivors. The *Nürnberg* would remain in dry dock for nearly five months; the *Leipzig* was so severely damaged that even after a year of repairs it could be used only as a training ship.

The unconventional policy of protecting destroyers with cruisers—condemned after the fact by Admiral Raeder as "inexpedient and wrong"—had proved costly. But Raeder and the navy suffered a much greater setback when they attempted to broaden the mine-laying campaign. Experiments had shown that the magnetic mines could be dropped not only from destroyers and U-boats, but also from aircraft by small parachutes. Raeder, elated by the successes achieved so far, urged the head of the Luftwaffe, Hermann Göring, to join in. Reluctantly, Göring did so, lending the navy a handful of obsolescent Heinkel 59 seaplanes based in the East Frisian Islands that could carry two mines each.

The first two aerial missions went satisfactorily, but the third, flown on the night of November 22, proved a disaster. Zooming low over the Thames estuary, one of the Heinkels deposited its pair of mines on a mud flat rather than in a channel. The mines were dropped near Shoeburyness, not far from a fully equipped Royal Navy workshop. In short order, a couple of British ordnance experts walked out to one of the mines, calmly defused it, and proceeded to unlock the precious secret of its magnetic detonating system. This was what the British had been waiting for. Within days, their experts were conjuring up countermeasures, devising ways to demagnetize the hulls of ships and developing shipboard devices that, radiating a magnetic field, detonated the mines at a safe distance.

German mine engineers ready a row of eight contact mines on the deck of a torpedo boat before sailing on a mine-laying mission. Each of the mines contained 330 pounds of explosives.

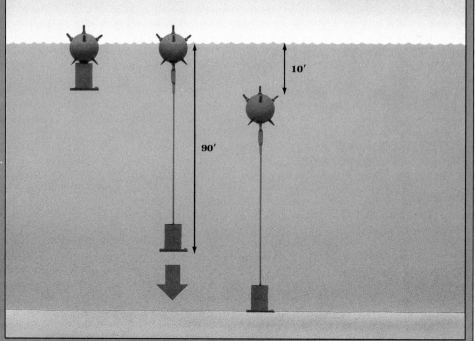

A contact mine attached to a pedestal anchor and coiled mooring cable flops into the sea from the fantail of a German warship. After the device hit the water and stabilized (*left*), its anchor separated and descended to the bottom, arming the mine and pulling it beneath the surface to a predetermined depth.

10'

90'

The Luftwaffe's blunder fueled Raeder's longstanding animosity toward Göring and his air force. The rift widened further two months later as the result of a grievous error in communications. On the night of February 22, 1940, six destroyers were steaming through a mine-swept channel in the West Wall to apprehend some British fishing trawlers that had been concentrating suspiciously in an area known as the Dogger Bank. Before the German ships had made it through the six-mile-wide channel, they were attacked by a twin-engine Heinkel 111 bomber whose pilot mistook them for enemy vessels. The bombs sank one destroyer, the *Leberecht Maass*, and damaged a second one, the *Max Schultz*, which then veered into a mine. Like the *Leberecht Maass* minutes before, the *Max Schultz* went down; a total of 578 men were lost from the two ships.

The navy was partly to blame for the tragedy. The Luftwaffe had told naval headquarters there would be a bombing mission that night against enemy shipping, but the navy had failed to warn its own destroyers about the raid and had also neglected to inform the Luftwaffe of the destroyers' foray against the British trawlers. What the incident really showed was the sad lack of cooperation between the navy and the air force. "It was," Raeder later said, "a costly demonstration of the folly of not placing all arms engaged in warfare at sea under unified command."

When operating without the Luftwaffe, the German destroyers racked up a remarkable record for safety and efficiency. During the four-month period ending on February 10, 1940, destroyer flotillas carried out eleven mine-laying missions without the loss of a single ship. And the 1,800 or so mines they had sown sank sixty-seven merchant vessels totaling 252,237 tons, as well as three British destroyers and six auxiliary warships. The German destroyers, in addition, had forced the British to divert vessels needed elsewhere to the dangerous task of clearing mines.

Admiral Raeder called a halt to the mine-laying campaign later that winter for several reasons. Unusually severe storms were endangering the destroyers, and the shorter nights of approaching spring were shrinking the periods of protective darkness. Most important, however, was the fact that the entire German fleet was soon to become involved in one of the boldest undertakings in naval history—the seaborne invasion of Norway.

Raeder had paid close attention to Norway and had frequently urged Hitler to consider the country's strategic importance. About one-third of the iron ore Germany imported from Sweden was carried by rail from the mines to the Norwegian port of Narvik, then shipped southward on German ore boats through a passage sailors call the Leads—a deepwater channel between the Norwegian mainland and a 1,200-mile-long offshore

chain of islands and reefs. The British, Raeder pointed out, most certainly had designs on Norway and on blocking this ore traffic. They might mine the Leads, or even invade and capture Narvik and other ports on the excuse of sending aid through them to Finland, which had recently been attacked by the Soviet Union. Besides wanting to protect this lifeline, Raeder coveted Norwegian ports as naval bases. Using those ports, German submarines and surface raiders could circumvent the developing British naval blockade, slipping out into the Atlantic to prey on British shipping.

Preoccupied with planning his moves on France and the Low Countries, Hitler was initially inclined to leave Norway alone as long as the country remained neutral and allowed German ships to pass through its coastal waters. As time went by, though, Hitler began to heed Raeder's warnings.

A British aerial photograph reveals the German supply ship *Altmark* at anchor in Norway's wintry Jössing Fjord. Alerted to the vessel's hiding place, the destroyer *Cossack* made a daring nighttime attack, rescuing British seamen held prisoner on board.

The clincher was an alarming British foray against a German vessel anchored in Norway's Jössing Fjord. The target was the supply ship *Altmark*, homeward bound from the South Atlantic where it had fueled and provisioned the pocket battleship *Graf Spee*. The British had learned that the *Altmark* carried British merchant seamen taken from ships sunk by the *Graf Spee*. On the night of February 16, a British destroyer, the *Cossack*, steamed into the fjord and sent a heavily armed party aboard the *Altmark*. In the hand-to-hand fight, seven German sailors were killed while the British liberated 299 of their countrymen. To the Germans, the raid on the *Altmark* seemed an outrageous and ominous violation of Norwegian neutrality. When Norway did nothing more than lodge a mild protest with London, Hitler decided to act.

Hitler approved the invasion plan, *Weserübung*—Weser Exercise— named after Germany's Weser River, on March 1. In response to Göring's desire to secure Danish airfields, the scheme called for the occupation of Denmark as well as Norway. German forces were to cooperate in a surprise assault from sea and air aimed at seizing eleven ports along a 1,000-mile front from the Danish capital of Copenhagen to the Norwegian city of Narvik, well above the Arctic Circle. At Raeder's suggestion, Weser Exercise was scheduled for the period of the new moon to guarantee dark nights for naval transit, and for early April, late enough to ensure that Germany's Baltic ports would be free of ice.

Rarely has a nation at war risked so much of its navy in one campaign. Raeder committed virtually his entire fleet—370 ships in all, from capital ships to merchantmen and minesweepers. While the *Scharnhorst* and the *Gneisenau*, along with a score of U-boats, protected against British intervention, eleven task forces made up of cruisers, destroyers, and smaller vessels would deliver more than 100,000 troops to the Scandinavian ports.

Some of the task forces would have to negotiate narrow fjords lined with formidable Norwegian gun installations. Ships assigned to the northernmost targets would have to travel almost 2,000 miles, exposed much of the way to attack by the Royal Navy and the RAF. Raeder admitted in a report to Hitler that such an operation was a gamble running "contrary to all principles in the theory of naval warfare." One of Raeder's deputies, Admiral Rolf Carls, anticipated losses of "about half the forces engaged."

The vanguard of the vast armada, consisting of supply vessels and tankers, left German bases on April 3; the task forces of warships began sailing three days later. Most of the landings took place on April 9 as planned. Some of them went with surprising smoothness. At Bergen the German force swiftly seized the port, although the light cruiser *Königsberg* took three hits from Norwegian coastal guns that crippled the ship's power and

In a mismatch off Norway, the 1,345-ton British destroyer *Glowworm* emerges from its own smoke screen just before turning to ram the 13,000-ton *Admiral Hipper*, whose swastika-blazoned bow is seen in the foreground.

steering systems. The port of Kristiansand also fell easily after a flight of Heinkel 111 bombers silenced its shore batteries. To the north, off the port of Trondheim, there had been trouble on April 8 when the heavy cruiser *Admiral Hipper* happened upon the British destroyer *Glowworm*. The destroyer had been participating in a mine-laying operation, the sort of action that Raeder had expected from the British. The *Hipper*, nearly ten times larger than the British vessel, bore down with its eight-inch guns blazing. The tiny *Glowworm*, on fire and unable to escape, turned and rammed the *Hipper*, ripping a 120-foot gash in the German vessel's armor plating. Despite the damage, the *Hipper* managed to rescue survivors from the sinking *Glowworm* and make its way to Trondheim. There, on April 9, the *Hipper* led four German destroyers into port, flashing Morse blinker signals in English that confused some of the Norwegian defenders. The shore batteries offered scant resistance, and Trondheim fell quickly.

The assault on the Norwegian capital of Oslo was, however, a different story. In the dim light before dawn, the heavy cruiser *Blücher* led a flotilla of sixteen vessels up the sixty-mile-long Oslo Fjord. The *Blücher*, newly commissioned, carried not only troops but also the nucleus of the occupation government to be installed in Oslo, complete with bureaucrats, filing cabinets, and stationery. As this floating model of Teutonic efficiency

reached a point about eighteen miles south of the capital, the fjord funneled into a passage less than 900 yards wide. On the island of Kaholmen to the left was the old Oscarsborg fortress, armed with batteries of eleven-inch guns. On the mainland to the right was another battery with a powerful searchlight that quickly caught the *Blücher* in its beam. "Suddenly, an earsplitting roar of thunder rends the air," wrote the *Blücher*'s Captain Kurt Zoepffel. "The glare of guns pierces the darkness. I can see three flashes simultaneously. We are under fire from two sides; the guns seem only 500 yards away. Soon bright flames are leaping from the ship."

Several shells from the fortress's big guns blasted the port side of the *Blücher* and the pocket battleship just behind it, the *Lützow*. The *Lützow* was the former *Deutschland*, renamed because Hitler feared the consequences to national morale if a ship named after Germany went down. The vessel saved itself by reversing engines and backing out of range with only its forward gun turret damaged. But the *Blücher*, its steering gear wrecked and its afterdeck an inferno of exploding ammunition and burning fuel, blundered ahead erratically. Just then, a pair of torpedoes fired from hidden launching tubes on the island smashed into the ship's engine room. Two hours later, the *Blücher* heeled over and sank. About 1,000 Germans died in the explosions and in the sea of flaming oil that surrounded the stricken ship. Some 1,300 survived, many of them soldiers who owed their lives to selfless sailors who, aware that the new *Blücher* was short of life jackets, gave their own to the troops as the ship went down.

Despite these terrible losses, the Germans took Oslo before the day was over. The *Lützow* and the other ships that had been following the *Blücher* backed down the fjord and managed to get their troops ashore. The soldiers then stormed the island fortress and moved on toward the city. Meanwhile, paratroopers and other airborne forces captured the city's airfield and swiftly deployed into the key government areas in Oslo's center.

From footholds up and down the Norwegian coast, Wehrmacht army units were soon moving inland against little opposition. But now the navy faced a race against time to get its warships headed home before they could be bottled up in the various fjords by a suddenly aroused British Home Fleet. The *Hipper*, for one, started moving southward from Trondheim on April 9, and that night barely escaped detection by a powerful Royal Navy flotilla of three battleships, an aircraft carrier, and three heavy cruisers. The *Scharnhorst* and the *Gneisenau* also sped for home early. Thanks to the opportune arrival of foul weather that concealed them, they were able to elude a force of no fewer than ninety-two RAF bombers.

Other vessels were less fortunate. The shell-crippled *Königsberg*, unable even to leave the pier at Bergen, took seven direct hits from British dive

bombers and became the first major warship ever to be sunk by hostile air action. Another one of the older, type-K cruisers, the *Karlsruhe*, was torpedoed and sunk by the enemy submarine *Truant* en route home from Kristiansand. The *Lützow*, sailing home from Oslo via the eastern edge of the Skagerrak on one of the shortest, safest routes of all, was damaged so severely by a torpedo from the submarine *Spearfish* that it had to be towed to port. It spent the next twelve months under repair.

It was in the far north, at Narvik, that German warships were hit the hardest after the invasion. Commodore Paul Friedrich Bonte, commander of the ten-destroyer flotilla there, had landed his ground forces as planned and was eager to get his ships home as soon as possible. He was frustrated, however, by fuel shortages; of the three tankers scheduled to refuel his vessels, only one had arrived. Norwegian guns had claimed one of the tankers, and heavy seas had delayed the other. On the morning of April 10, all of Bonte's destroyers remained in the waters near Narvik, five of them inside the constricted harbor itself.

At dawn that morning, five British destroyers of the II Flotilla approached Narvik through the Vest Fjord, one of several passages to the harbor. In the dim light, they made their way unseen through fog and falling snow past a screen of U-boats intended to prevent such intrusions. Inside the harbor, the intruders caught the German destroyers napping and rudely awakened them with salvos of shells and torpedoes. The alarm had scarcely been sounded on the German flagship *Wilhelm Heidkamp* when a torpedo tore away its stern, killing Commodore Bonte and most of his staff. A pair of torpedoes broke the *Anton Schmitt* in half. Two other German destroyers, the *Diether von Roeder* and the *Hans Lüdemann*, were severely damaged by shellfire. Less than an hour after their surreptitious entrance, the British retired into the main fjord, leaving a harbor littered with sunken, sinking, and battered German destroyers. As the British departed, they dispatched six German merchant vessels anchored in the harbor.

Although the British destroyer force withdrew still practically unscratched, trouble awaited them. The five remaining German destroyers, deployed in the branching side fjords, steamed out to pounce upon the British flotilla. With two ships in front of the British and three in the rear, the German warships poured out a savage cross fire of shells and torpedoes, swiftly knocking out two of the enemy destroyers, including the flagship *Hardy*. Aboard the *Hardy*, the flotilla commander, Captain B. A. W. Warburton-Lee, was killed less than two hours after his German counterpart, Commodore Bonte.

The three British survivors limped away under the cover of a snowstorm. Though damaged, one of them, the *Havock*, was still able to land two

Capsized and burning, the German heavy cruiser *Blücher* lies in the narrow Oslo Fjord after being hit by Norwegian gunfire and torpedoes. After capturing Oslo, the Germans erected a memorial *(right)* to the soldiers and sailors who had died in the *Blücher* catastrophe for "Führer and fatherland."

high-explosive shells on a cargo ship, the *Rauenfels*, blowing up the vessel and most of the ammunition meant for the German troops now ashore at Narvik. Out in the Vest Fjord, the British sailed by the U-25 and the U-51, two of the submarines that had failed to note their entrance earlier that morning. The U-boats saw the British destroyers this time and fired torpedoes. But, as happened with alarming frequency throughout the Norwegian campaign, the torpedoes malfunctioned, detonating prematurely.

The German navy's troubles at Narvik were anything but over. Three days later the British returned in greater strength—nine destroyers and the 30,600-ton battleship *Warspite*—to take on the reduced German defenders. As a Swordfish seaplane catapulted from the *Warspite* scouted ahead, the British flotilla steamed into Narvik with all guns firing. First they found the destroyer *Erich Koellner*, badly mauled in the previous battle, lurking in

Curious Norwegian civilians eye German naval vessels docked in Oslo harbor near the city hall (background) shortly after the invasion. Some Norwegians accepted the German occupation calmly, but an active resistance movement sabotaged German installations in Norway throughout the war.

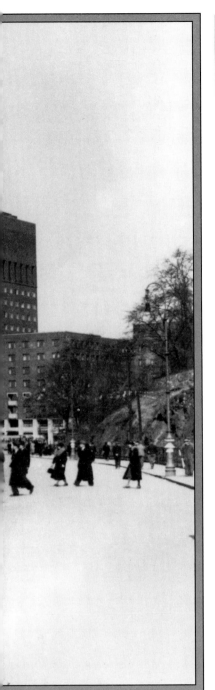

ambush in a side fjord and pounded it to pieces. Sailing on, the British hunted down the remaining seven German vessels one by one, relentlessly pursuing those that tried to escape in the web of fjords.

By midafternoon only a single German destroyer, the *Georg Thiele*, remained in action. It was cornered in the Rombakken Fjord with two torpedoes left in its tubes. The first, fired by mistake, exploded harmlessly against some rocks; the second blew away the bow of the British destroyer *Eskimo*. But that was the *Georg Thiele*'s last gallant gasp. With no ammunition left, the captain gave up the struggle, ordering that the *Georg Thiele* be run aground and abandoned. By late afternoon, the impressive German flotilla that had landed the troops at Narvik only four days previously was nothing more than scrap metal.

The naval battles at Narvik were considered heroic defeats in Germany, and special medals were struck commemorating them. But the only real benefit the Germans derived from the two engagements came in the form of reinforcements for the ground forces in the Narvik area. More than 2,000 surviving sailors were rounded up by Narvik's army commander, Brigadier General Eduard Dietl, and formed into infantry brigades. As it happened, these sailors-turned-soldiers would be sorely needed. They joined with the infantry in resisting the advance of a combined force of British, French, and Polish troops bent on retaking Narvik. The Allies succeeded in occupying the port on May 27, but Dietl's troops hung on grimly in the mountains nearby. When the Allies, deeming their position untenable, abandoned Narvik on June 8, the Germans marched back into the port.

Elsewhere, Allied landings aimed at recapturing Trondheim and other German footholds were plagued by a lack of coordination, and none succeeded. The Royal Navy had to pluck the expeditionary troops off the rocky Norwegian coast and ferry them back to England.

The Allied retreat from Narvik, already a triumph for the Germans, gave Admiral Raeder a chance to rack up a victory at sea. Sailing in the open Atlantic west of Narvik, Raeder's twin battleships, the *Scharnhorst* and the *Gneisenau*, came across the British aircraft carrier *Glorious* escorted by only two destroyers. Conditions were ideal for a German attack. Visibility was sharp, and the *Glorious* was steaming along at a snail's pace, its flight deck crammed with its own forty-eight aircraft plus a number of RAF fighters that had flown off the Norwegian mainland.

The German battleships, with their forward guns almost fully elevated, began firing from a range of more than 28,000 yards—nearly sixteen miles. Their aim was nearly perfect. Before the *Glorious* could launch a single plane, shells had smashed its flight deck, their impact prying open large sections of the steel plating "like the lid of a box," according to the German

commander, Admiral Wilhelm Marschall. The carrier and its two destroyers soon went down under a barrage so unrelenting that the *Scharnhorst* alone fired 212 shells. But the *Scharnhorst*'s stern was seriously damaged by a torpedo fired from one of the *Glorious*'s sinking escorts. A few days later, the *Gneisenau*'s bow was holed by a torpedo from a British submarine. The two German ships would have to spend weeks in dry dock for repairs. Still, they had succeeded in sinking one of Britian's precious carriers and weakening the Royal Navy's command in the North Sea.

The entire Norwegian campaign, in fact, amounted to a huge victory. To be sure, Raeder's navy had lost heavily—three cruisers, ten destroyers, four U-boats, and assorted other vessels. Nonetheless, both Raeder and his Führer regarded the losses as a fair price for the Reich's gains. The Germans had secured their northern flank, insured the flow of iron ore from Sweden, and captured a string of strategically located naval bases from which to strike blows at the Royal Navy.

Meanwhile, the focus of Hitler's war was shifting to the south, where events were eclipsing the Norwegian campaign. On May 10, Hitler had launched his invasion of the Low Countries and France. The collapse of France on June 22, fourteen days after the Allied withdrawal from Norway, allowed Raeder to select home bases for his U-boats and surface ships in hospitable coastal regions south of the British Isles.

The British Admiralty now faced vastly increased odds. The capitulation of their French allies left the British to fight on alone at sea. Moreover, Italy's entry into the war brought an entire new fleet to contend with in the Mediterranean. Stretched to the breaking point, the Royal Navy could maintain only the thinnest of picket lines to challenge whatever raiders the Germans sent to attack Allied merchant shipping.

To take advantage of these changed fortunes, Admiral Raeder was forced to rely for some time on a another weapon in his high-seas arsenal. The Norwegian campaign had cost his surface fleet, in addition to the outright losses, the services of a number of vessels, including two pocket battleships, two battleships, two cruisers, and six destroyers, all damaged and temporarily out of action. Only three cruisers and four destroyers were in condition to go to sea, and even this meager force was immobilized during the summer of 1940, waiting to take part in Operation Sea Lion, Hitler's abortive cross-channel invasion of England.

Raeder's new weapons were *Hilfskreuzer*, or auxiliary cruisers, former freighters converted into armed raiders. Some of these vessels were slightly larger than the average merchantman, most were somewhat faster, and all were armed to the teeth with half a dozen 5.9-inch guns and two to six

A foundered and smoking merchant vessel rests in the harbor of Narvik after a German destroyer force seized the port on April 9, 1940. Retaliatory raids by the Royal Navy on April 10 and 13 wiped out the German invasion flotilla, including the two destroyers moored to a dock in the foreground.

Its bow in the air, the British troopship *Orama* plunges toward the bottom off Narvik on June 8, 1940, as a German destroyer

stands by to pick up survivors. To the Germans' dismay, the *Orama* carried German prisoners of war rather than British troops.

torpedo tubes. They also carried one or two seaplanes for reconnaissance. The powerful weaponry was carefully concealed in fake deckhouses and behind sliding panels and hinged bulkheads. Even viewed from quite close, the ships looked utterly innocent, like ordinary tramp steamers. They usually flew the flags of neutral nations and disguised themselves accordingly. They carried large stores of paint and quick-change props such as telescopic funnels and pieces of fake superstructure so they could alter their color and shape—several times if necessary—during a voyage.

The raiders' tactics, perfected by their predecessors in World War I, resembled those of marauding pirate ships in centuries past. Approaching an unsuspecting merchantman that might be carrying goods valuable to Britain's war effort, a raider would fire a warning shot across the bow. If the merchantman was armed and tried to resist, the raider would attempt to sink it on the spot with gunfire or a torpedo. If the merchant vessel hove to, the German raider would order the crew off, then scuttle or sink the ship. At times, if the merchantman's cargo was of high value to the Reich, the German captain would put a prize crew aboard to sail the vessel back to an Axis port. The captive crew would either be sent toward the nearest harbor in lifeboats or be taken aboard the raider to be transferred to one of the supply ships that provisioned and fueled the raider fleet.

The raiders normally stayed at sea for more than a year at a time. They replenished fuel and other supplies from captured vessels when they were able to, and they rendezvoused with their supply ships as directed by coded radio message from naval headquarters in Germany. Occasionally they met one another at sea to swap booty and information. Meanwhile, the captains fought the boredom of the long voyages by providing movies or arranging amateur theatricals.

Three of the auxiliary cruisers slipped out of German ports before the campaign in Norway was over; four more sailed before the end of 1940. These seven ships, like the two more that followed, fanned out into the Atlantic and beyond to disrupt the flow of war materials and food—rubber, oil, grain, and other vital commodities—to Britain from the outposts of the empire. From 1940 through 1943, they sank or captured no fewer than 142 vessels totaling nearly 900,000 tons.

The first of the raiders, the *Atlantis*, sailed from Kiel on March 31, 1940, with a crew of 347 men under Captain Bernhard Rogge, a respected forty-year-old veteran of World War I. The *Atlantis* began the cruise disguised as the *Krim*, an auxiliary warship of the then-neutral Soviet Union. But like the other raiders to follow, the *Atlantis* was ready to swap identities at any time, with Captain Rogge choosing as his model any vessel of similar size and basic configuration listed in Lloyd's Register of Shipping.

Victim of a British submarine attack, the German pocket battleship *Lützow* sits in a slip at Kiel before going to dry dock, its entire stern section cracked, dangling, and awash. The ship was hit by a torpedo on the return home from Norway.

After a couple of weeks in the North Atlantic, the *Atlantis* turned southward, crossed the equator, and took on a new identity. Knowing that few Russian warships could be expected in such southerly waters, Captain Rogge had his vessel transformed with paint and props into the Japanese cargo-and-passenger ship *Kasii Maru*. Rogge wrote later that the ruse even extended to some playacting by members of the crew: "Bespectacled dark-haired sailors, wearing white head scarves and shirts outside their trousers, could be seen moving about the decks. A 'woman' was pushing a pram; on the boat deck six 'Japanese passengers' lay in deck chairs. All was ready for our first victim."

On May 3, in the busy shipping lane between Cape Town and Freetown along the west coast of Africa, a target came into view. It was the British cargo ship *Scientist*, en route from Durban, South Africa, to Liverpool, carrying grain, hides, copper, and chromium. Rogge closed in that afternoon, hoisted the German naval ensign in place of the bogus Rising Sun flag, and signaled the *Scientist* to heave to. When the British showed no sign of obeying, he gave the order to his crew, "Uncover the guns!"

The *Atlantis* opened fire from a range of about two and a half miles, the gunners aiming the first shots wide as a warning. But when the *Scientist* steamed away at full speed, the 5.9-inch guns zeroed in. Shells struck the merchantman's stern, then the bridge, and finally hit amidships, setting the ship aflame and sending the crew to the lifeboats. Before the radio was put out of action, the wounded operator managed to transmit the alarm signal QQQ—"I am being attacked by an unidentified enemy ship." It was a distress call that would become dishearteningly familiar to the British

during the following months. Having taken aboard all survivors—and some documents that would help him mimic the color schemes of British merchant ships—Rogge dispatched the flaming hulk with a torpedo.

Rogge's reputation for treating merchant crewmen and other survivors fairly was put to the test in the South Atlantic on the night of April 16, 1941, when he spotted a ship sailing suspiciously without lights. The vessel was, in fact, the Egyptian liner *Zamzam*, carrying 202 civilian passengers. Rogge, however, mistook it for an old British troop transport that, like his own ship, had been converted into an armed merchant cruiser. Thinking he was facing an enemy vessel, Rogge fired without warning and quickly disabled the *Zamzam*. He soon realized his mistake, however, and took care to rescue all the passengers and crew, who were then transferred to the German freighter *Dresden* and taken to occupied France.

Rogge's magnanimity proved to be his ship's undoing, however. Two American journalists had been aboard the *Zamzam*, and their account of the drama at sea, published in *Life* magazine, brought wide notoriety to the secret raiders. The magazine's photograph of the *Atlantis* was soon hanging in the wardroom of every British warship. Later that year, the crew of the armed merchant cruiser *Devonshire* consulted the picture to confirm their identification of the *Atlantis* before sinking it. Rogge and most of his crew were rescued by U-boats. The *Atlantis* had made an extraordinarily long and profitable voyage. At sea for 622 days, the ship had steamed 112,500 miles and had sunk or captured twenty-two ships totaling 146,000 tons.

Five raiders followed the *Atlantis* to sea one after the other during the spring and early summer of 1940: the *Orion*, the *Widder*, the *Thor*, the *Pinguin*, and finally the *Komet*. Undoubtedly the *Komet* undertook the most arduous passage. Heading north into the Arctic, the small ship turned eastward and sailed 3,300 miles across the top of Russia, negotiating the semifrozen Kara Sea with the help of a pair of Soviet icebreakers. Passing north of Siberia, the *Komet* then ducked down through the Bering Strait to begin its raiding career in the Pacific.

The most successful of the raiders, however, was the *Pinguin*, a well-armed vessel of 7,776 tons brilliantly commanded by a twenty-five-year navy veteran named Ernst-Felix Krüder. Daring and resourceful, Krüder was especially inventive in his use of the ship's seaplanes, employing them not only to scout out victims but also to silence their radios. A prime danger for all the German raiders was a victim's QQQ distress signal, for it could quickly bring hostile warships or aircraft rushing to the scene. Krüder's novel solution was to have a seaplane—wearing British markings—zoom over a merchant ship's masts and rip away its radio antennae with a grapnel before the radioman realized what was happening. Using this

The Many Faces of the Orion

Assisted by a tug, the *Orion* steams out of icy Kiel harbor emitting smoke from its real and false stacks. The auxiliary cruiser's cargo consisted of tons of paint and structural material used to facilitate quick changes in its appearance.

As the surface raider *Orion* sailed from Kiel on March 30, 1940, disguised as a two-funneled naval auxiliary, seaman Paul Schmidt sat cramped inside the phony rear stack. His assignment was to produce smoke by tossing oily rags into a small furnace.

Before the *Orion* had gone far, however, Schmidt and his nimble mates disassembled the second stack and the dummy wooden guns on the ship's deck. Working fast while under way, they transformed the dull gray auxiliary into a replica of the Holland America Line's freighter *Beemsterdijk*, complete with green and white funnel bands, a yellow hull stripe, white upper works, and a black hull.

These were only the first of at least twenty false identities the *Orion* would assume on a marathon voyage of 510 days and 127,337 miles, the greatest distance logged by any of Germany's far-flung raiders. With an actor's flair, Captain Kurt Weyher used his trove of many-colored paints, tarpaulins, bogus flags, improvised uniforms, and fake masts to change the *Orion's* visage and confound its pursuers. The raider's real guns were cleverly masked as cargo, cranes, hatch covers, or deckhouses to give the ship the innocuous look of a noncombatant as it approached to within point-blank range of its unsuspecting victims.

The chameleon was never apprehended, and before returning to port in August 1941, it sank or captured 73,000 tons of Allied shipping.

1

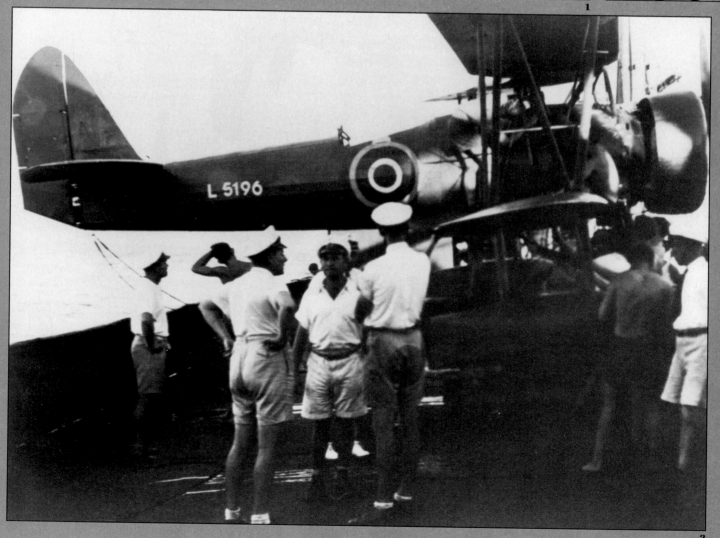

3

1 Before its conversion to a navy auxiliary cruiser, the *Orion* plied Atlantic trade routes as an unarmed freighter *(above, left)*.

2 Sailors secure the hinged plates that conceal the *Orion's* guns *(above)*. The steel flaps could be dropped in seconds as the *Orion* prepared to threaten or fire on another ship.

3 In January 1941, the *Orion* received a Nakajima 90-11 scout plane *(left)* painted with the roundel insignia of the RAF.

4 Lashed-down tarpaulins *(right)* hide the *Orion's* stern guns. The ship's armament consisted of six 5.9-inch guns, six anti-aircraft guns, two 75-mm guns, and six torpedo tubes.

technique, Krüder safely executed an incredible triple play off Madagascar on August 26, 1940, sinking two tankers and a freighter in a matter of hours. Before its raiding voyages ended, the *Pinguin* claimed twenty-eight Allied vessels, sunk or captured.

Perhaps the most pugnacious of the German raiders was the *Thor*, which showed its mettle by sinking six merchant vessels within a month after emerging into the open Atlantic in mid-June 1940. Captain Otto Kähler and his crew earned their reputation for aggressiveness by dueling with armed merchant cruisers that the Royal Navy had sent to sea, even though they were larger than the *Thor* and equally well armed.

The first battle occurred on July 28 as the *Thor* steamed along about 600 miles off the coast of Brazil. Suddenly, over the horizon appeared the British merchant cruiser *Alcantara*, which quickly turned toward the *Thor* and began to give chase. At first the *Thor* ran for it, but the British ship, faster as well as bigger, began to catch up. Finally Kähler realized that his only hope was to turn and fight it out. When the range fell to 14,000 yards, he opened fire, and the two vessels traded salvos for thirty minutes. The *Thor* took two hits, but the British gunners had to peer into a bright sun and their aim proved erratic. Soon the *Thor*'s fire began to tell. Shells found the *Alcantara*'s engine room, and the ship came to a halt, dead in the water. Now that escape was possible, Captain Kähler quickly steamed away.

Kähler and his men went on to slug it out with two more armed merchant ships over the next nine months, mauling one enemy vessel so severely that it had to put into Montevideo to be patched with steel plates salvaged from the wreck of the scuttled German pocket battleship *Graf Spee*. The other British merchant cruiser took such a pounding that at length it foundered.

Proud as they were of such exploits, raider captains realized that they and their ships lived on borrowed time. Captain Theodor Detmers of the *Kormoran* allowed his exuberant young officers to paint the names of the ship's victims on the bulkhead of the wardroom because he did not want to dampen their enthusiasm. But he knew that on any day his own ship might be the victim. "Every wisp of smoke, every mast top could have spelled the end," he said later, "and although a raider captain soon learned to live with that concept, it was still a fact that could not be escaped."

In the autumn of 1940, Admiral Raeder was able to bring fresh weapons to bear in the campaign against British shipping. The indefinite postponement in September of Operation Sea Lion, the invasion of England, had released his diminished fleet of warships for new duties. For all the havoc being wrought by the six merchant raiders then at sea—by the end of

October, they already had accounted for forty Allied vessels—these marauders were intended to operate against ships sailing alone. Raeder wanted to take on bigger game: the convoys increasingly being employed by the British to negotiate the Atlantic safely. During the next six months, Raeder would deploy an impressive quartet of capital ships in the pursuit of convoys: three battleships and a heavy cruiser.

The first of these warships to set out for an extended cruise that autumn was the pocket battleship *Admiral Scheer*. Fitted with a sleek new fighting mast containing the latest radio, radar, and fire-control equipment, the *Scheer* slipped out into the North Sea at the end of October and headed up the coast of Norway. Then, under cover of a storm so violent it swept two men overboard, the battleship made its way unseen into the Atlantic through the Denmark Strait between Greenland and Iceland, becoming the first major German warship to reach the open ocean since the *Scheer*'s sister ship, the *Graf Spee*, nearly a year before.

By the morning of November 5, the *Scheer* was in mid-Atlantic, athwart the main convoy route between North America and England. Captain Theodor Krancke launched one of the ship's two Arado seaplanes. German naval intelligence had reported a large convoy eastbound from the Canadian port of Halifax. Lieutenant Pietsch, at the controls of the aircraft, found the convoy some three hours' steaming time to the south and flew back to flash the news with Morse light signals.

Captain Krancke set course for the convoy at full speed ahead, twenty-eight knots. About half past two in the afternoon, he came upon a British merchant vessel, the *Mopan*, but it was sailing alone and evidently not part of the convoy. Krancke ordered the merchantman to stop and sent three warning shots across its deck. The crew immediately abandoned ship. The *Mopan* was a refrigerator ship, and ordinarily Krancke would have put a crew aboard to take it home. But he was in a hurry. The *Scheer* sank the British vessel, rescued the crew, and hurried on southward.

Shortly before half past four, a lookout saw a smudge of smoke on the horizon, then a forest of masts. It was convoy HX84, thirty-seven assorted merchantmen escorted by a single armed merchant cruiser, the *Jervis Bay*. As the *Scheer* bore down on the convoy, the escort emerged from the pack. It laid down a smoke screen to shield the convoy, sent up red Very signals ordering the ships to scatter, and charged directly at the *Scheer*. The captain of the *Jervis Bay*, E. S. F. Fegen, was deliberately sacrificing his ship in hopes of allowing the others to escape.

At a distance of more than ten miles, well beyond the range of the *Jervis Bay*'s six-inchers, Krancke's six 11-inch guns began blasting away. The first four salvos bracketed the target; then the shells began to find their mark,

setting the British ship afire and knocking out most of its guns. Still the *Jervis Bay* came on, steaming straight at the battleship. An early hit cost Captain Fegen one of his legs, and he soon suffered a severe injury to the other. Nevertheless, with the help of the ship's surgeon he was able to direct the fire of his last remaining gun, which kept blasting until the British vessel had closed to within a mile of the *Scheer.* Then, perforated stem to stern, the *Jervis Bay* went down with Captain Fegen and 200 members of his crew. Their bravery had given the rest of the convoy a twenty-two-minute head start in the gathering darkness.

The *Scheer* sped through the fading light and billowing smoke screens generated by the scattered merchantmen. Employing radar, searchlights, and star shells, Krancke and his crew found one ship after another, setting them aflame with well-directed fire. Before breaking off the hunt at 8:40 that evening with half of its ammunition used up, the *Scheer* had dispatched five merchantmen and damaged three others.

The toll was not as great as it might have been without the *Jervis Bay*'s gallant delaying action. But the *Scheer*'s attack on convoy HX84 still prompted a massive overhaul of British convoy arrangements. All merchant sailings in the North Atlantic were suspended for a week, and two convoys already eastbound from Canada were recalled to Halifax. For months afterward, the British seldom let a big convoy sail without a battleship or a couple of cruisers as escort, which proved a steady drain on the Royal Navy and played right into Raeder's hands. With one swift blow the *Scheer* had handsomely fulfilled Raeder's instructions. What he wanted, he said, was "not necessarily a heavy toll of ships, but maximum disorganization of the enemy's supply and convoy systems."

To block the *Scheer*'s expected return to port, the British sent out forces almost as large as the entire German navy—two battleships, two battle cruisers, three regular cruisers, and six destroyers. But Captain Krancke had no intention of curtailing his successful sortie. Easily evading his British pursuers, he headed south, crossed the equator, and, on December 18, captured a fortuitous prize for the holiday season—the British refrigerator ship *Duquesa* with a cornucopia of fruits and vegetables, 3,500 tons of frozen meat, and about 15 million eggs. The *Scheer*'s crewmen feasted the next day on uncommon provender stylishly served by British stewards in white jackets. A week later, they shared their bounty at a Christmas rendezvous with the raider *Thor* and three tanker-supply ships in the middle of the South Atlantic, some 6,000 miles from home.

Thanks in part to the *Duquesa*, the *Scheer* now enjoyed a resupply system second to none among warships at sea. The German tanker *Nordmark* met the pocket battleship regularly to replenish its fuel. And after the

A member of a prize crew from the *Admiral Scheer* hauls down the British Union Jack on board the refrigerated cargo ship *Duquesa*, captured on December 18, 1940. The *Duquesa*'s prodigious bounty of foodstuffs helped supply half a dozen German ships at sea.

Duquesa ran out of coal for its old-fashioned boilers, the tanker towed it slowly around the South Atlantic to serve as a floating larder for the *Scheer* and other German ships, including the raiders *Atlantis* and *Pinguin*. The German prize crew on the *Duquesa* meanwhile ripped out all the vessel's woodwork and burned it to keep the refrigerator system running.

In the South Atlantic and the Indian Ocean, Krancke tried a variation on the tricks used by the *Thor* and the other raiders, painting the *Scheer* to look like a British cruiser and further disguising it by lowering the middle gun of each of its two turrets. Krancke then approached unsuspecting merchantmen in daylight and persuaded them to stop by emulating British signaling procedures. This usually enabled the Germans to capture the ship before it could send a radio alert and betray the *Scheer*'s position.

The deception proved so effective that by the time the *Scheer* was ordered home in March 1941 it had sunk or captured a total of seventeen vessels and had led British warships on a frustrating chase on both sides of the equator. On March 30, Krancke's forty-eighth birthday, the *Scheer* dropped anchor at the Norwegian port of Bergen, completing 161 days at sea and the most successful voyage of the war by a regular German warship operating alone. Two days later, the ship reached its home port of Kiel and was personally welcomed by Admiral Raeder. The officers' mess proudly

The new heavy cruiser *Prinz Eugen* (background) lies at a dock in Kiel in the spring of 1941 before sailing to join the battleship *Bismarck* for a sortie into the Atlantic. The ship's departure from the Baltic Sea harbor was delayed after it hit a mine—probably laid by the Royal Air Force—during a sea trial and sustained damage to its fuel bunkers, propeller shafts, and electrical system.

hosted the grand admiral at a lunch of steaks smothered with eggs—"an involuntary gift," Krancke explained, "from Mr. Winston Churchill."

While the *Scheer* was at sea during the fall and winter of 1940-41, three other German warships were staging raids on British shipping. One was the heavy cruiser *Admiral Hipper*. Damaged during the Norway invasion, it had since been repaired but still suffered from engine trouble. Nevertheless, the *Hipper* returned to the Atlantic briefly in February and scored heavily, sinking seven merchantmen totaling 32,086 tons during an attack on an unescorted convoy 200 miles east of the Azores. The *Hipper*'s engines soon acted up, however, and the cruiser was forced to retreat to the French port of Brest, then to a dry dock at Kiel for a thorough overhaul.

The twin battleships *Gneisenau* and *Scharnhorst* also broke out into the Atlantic. Patched up like the *Hipper* after the Norwegian campaign, the two vessels went to sea in tandem under one of Raeder's most trusted senior officers, Admiral Günther Lütjens. During a two-day period in mid-March, Lütjens's force sank sixteen ill-protected merchantmen. A week later, on March 22, the battleships sailed triumphantly into Brest, having disposed of twenty-two vessels displacing nearly 116,000 tons.

The first three months of 1941 marked the zenith of Raeder's surface campaign against British commerce. It was the surface fleet's equivalent of what the U-boat crews referred to as *die glückliche Zeit*—"the happy time." In January, February, and March, the four heavy warships and the six disguised raiders accounted for no less than sixty-two ships totaling 302,567 tons. This amounted to more than half the toll exacted meanwhile by Admiral Dönitz's thirty U-boats. In March alone, the combined British losses to both surface and submarine attacks reached 350,000 tons, a new high for the war and a rate Britain could not long survive.

But soon a troubling series of setbacks afflicted the German fleet. In early April, the *Scharnhorst* was laid up with engine problems that turned out to be more serious than expected. On April 6, the *Gneisenau*, riding at anchor in the harbor at Brest, took a torpedo in the stern from an RAF Beaufort aircraft and was out of action for more than six months. On April 23, plans to send the newly commissioned heavy cruiser *Prinz Eugen* to sea were delayed when the ship, steaming on its shakedown cruise in the Baltic, hit a mine and was laid up for two weeks.

Then, on May 8 in the Indian Ocean, the unparalleled voyage of the merchant raider *Pinguin* came to an abrupt end after nearly eleven months. Attacked by the British cruiser *Cornwall*, the *Pinguin* exploded and sank with its captain and most of its crew. The loss of the ship, the first of the auxiliary cruisers to go down, was yet another warning that the surface fleet's happy time might soon be ending. ✚

A Sea Wolf in Lamb's Dress

Captain Ernst-Felix Krüder *(above)* had worked his way up from seaman in the German navy before he took over the auxiliary cruiser HK-33 *(right)*, which he renamed the *Pinguin*. Assuming many guises under Krüder's command, the *Pinguin* traveled 59,000 miles—or more than twice around the world—and sank or captured twenty-eight Allied merchant ships *(see map, below)*.

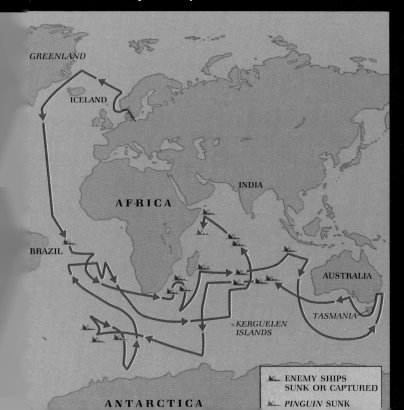

GREENLAND

ICELAND

INDIA

AFRICA

BRAZIL

AUSTRALIA

TASMANIA

KERGUELEN
ISLANDS

ANTARCTICA

| | ENEMY SHIPS SUNK OR CAPTURED |
| | PINGUIN SUNK |

When the 7,700-ton freighter *Kandelfels* was launched at the port of Bremen in 1936, neither its designer nor its crew could have imagined that this innocuous merchant vessel would become for a time one of the most feared warships on the high seas. Early in 1940, the humble *Kandelfels* was transformed into *Hilfskreuzer 33*, one of nine so-called auxiliary cruisers pressed into service by the short-handed German navy.

Auxiliary cruisers were warships in disguise, raiders whose mission was to capture or destroy Allied merchant vessels. Although their officers came mostly from

the merchant marine and their crews were navy enlisted men, they improvised a grab bag of costumes, and the ships themselves had the harmless look of noncombatants. The HK-33's armament—six 5.9-inch guns, seven antiaircraft weapons, and four torpedo tubes—was carefully camouflaged. Concealed in the hold were crates of ammunition, 300 mines, and two small scout planes. An ingenious system of raising and lowering phony masts and smokestacks, a collection of foreign flags, and a selection of different colored paints enabled the HK-33 to assume the profile, color

scheme, and nationality of authentic neutral vessels.

The HK-33 put to sea on June 15, 1940, commanded by Captain Ernst-Felix Krüder, an imperturbable disciplinarian who had served in the German Imperial Navy during World War I. Krüder betrayed a sense of wry humor when he gave his new ship the decidedly unwarlike name *Pinguin*, or Penguin, noting that one species of the deceptively awkward-looking little bird "steals the eggs of the others." Over the next eleven months, the *Pinguin* would sink or capture more Allied ships than any other German surface vessel.

Boldly marked as the Greek
freighter *Kassos*, the *Pinguin*
stands off while its sailors use
rubber rafts to ferry supplies to
the submarine *UA (foreground)*.

A Friendly Atlantic Rendezvous

In addition to its offensive mission, the *Pinguin* occasionally resupplied conventional German warships, thus prolonging the time they could spend at sea. While roving the Atlantic disguised as a Greek freighter in July of 1940, the *Pinguin* rendezvoused near the equator with the German submarine *UA*. The U-boat was low on provisions and had exhausted its supply of torpedoes in attacks on Allied ships. Over a period of seven days, the *Pinguin* successfully transferred food, fuel, and torpedoes to the *UA*, marking the first time that a surface raider had refueled and rearmed a submarine at sea.

At left, the British freighter *Benavon* burns off Madagascar after being shelled by the *Pinguin* on September 12, 1940. The captain and several officers went down with the ship, which was bound for London from Manila carrying hemp and rubber.

At left, below, the freighter *Morviken*, pride of Norway's merchant fleet, sinks in the Indian Ocean after its encounter with the *Pinguin*. The Norwegians had sailed under a British charter since the German invasion a few months earlier.

Prisoners crowd the deck of the *Storstad*, a Norwegian tanker that was waylaid by the *Pinguin* on October 7, 1940, off the northwest coast of Australia. Captain Krüder decided to convert the captured ship into an auxiliary minelayer.

Raider on a Rampage

On July 31, 1940, the *Pinguin* claimed its first victim. Approaching the British freighter *Domingo de Larrinaga* off the coast of Africa, the raider fired three warning shots, then riddled the freighter with shellfire. A German boarding party evacuated the crew, and the *Pinguin* sank the ship with a torpedo.

After rounding the Cape of Good Hope and sailing into the Indian Ocean, the *Pinguin* accounted for three more Allied vessels in the space of eight hours from August 26 to 27. On September 16, it forced the surrender of the Norwegian freighter *Nordvard.* Rather than sink the ship and its cargo of grain, Krüder sent it to Germany carrying 150 prisoners and bags of mail for the families of the *Pinguin*'s crew.

Wearing regulation hats and informal clothing, three of the *Pinguin*'s officers *(upper left)* take charge of the *Passat (above)* in its new career as a minelayer.

The Making of a Minelayer

Using a hoist normally employed to drop scout planes into the water, German sailors gingerly lower one of the *Pinguin*'s mines into a captured motorboat that has been lined with mattresses to cushion the landing.

In three days, Krüder's crew converted the tanker *Storstad* into a minelayer and gave it the docile name *Passat*, or Trade Wind.

Transferring the mines at sea was a ticklish business. The *Pinguin*'s rubber rafts proved incapable of carrying them, so they were loaded instead aboard a sturdy motorboat salvaged from an earlier victim.

Manned by Germans from the *Pinguin*, the *Passat* scattered its mines in the busy sea lanes between Tasmania and the Australian mainland, and they soon sank several ships. One, the *City of Rayville*, was the first American vessel lost to hostile action in the war.

recalled the *Pinguin*'s surgeon, Dr. Werner Hasselmann. For two days the sailors braved high seas in small boats to exchange visits, gifts, and tales of their adventures. Then the raiders went their separate ways.

Rough water separates the auxiliary cruiser *Atlantis* *(background)* from the *Pinguin* at their rendezvous in the Indian Ocean. Although the *Pinguin* captured or destroyed more enemy ships than any other raider, the *Atlantis* spent a record time at sea: 622 days.

The *Pinguin's* motor launch approaches the *Pelagos,* one of three factory ships that processed the whales taken by the fleet. Each factory ship employed more than 200 sailors.

With its battle flag flying (*upper right*), the *Pinguin* escorts the captive Norwegian whaling fleet to a meeting in the South Atlantic with a German supply ship, from which Krüder hoped to requisition enough sailors to provide crews for his prizes.

Capturing
a Fleet
of Whalers

Under guard, the Norwegian whalers continue hunting and processing their catch (*below*). They used the whales' huge carcasses as fenders to cushion collisions between the whaling ships and the factory vessels.

When Captain Bernhard Rogge of the raider *Atlantis* presented Captain Krüder with a set of confiscated Norwegian whaling maps, Krüder decided to take the *Pinguin* south to Antarctica in search of new prey: the Norwegian whaling fleet.

In mid-January 1941, Krüder came upon the vulnerable fleet, and in two days the *Pinguin*—without firing a shot—seized eleven whalers and three factory ships containing 22,000 tons of whale oil. The captured sailors obeyed Krüder's instructions to pursue business as usual and finished their rendering of the whale carcasses before steaming north under prize crews. All but two of the vessels arrived safely at Bordeaux in German-occupied France.

At left, above, the eight-inch guns of the *Cornwall* respond with a salvo after the *Pinguin*, choosing not to surrender, fired the first shots of the encounter.

At left, a shell from the *Pinguin* explodes short of its mark. The *Cornwall*, after taking a direct hit, had maneuvered beyond range of the *Pinguin*'s 5.9-inch guns.

At top, a huge explosion consumes the *Pinguin*. Twelve minutes into the engagement, the *Cornwall*'s guns scored four hits on the *Pinguin*, and one of the shells ignited 130 mines stored on the German ship.

When the Pirate's Luck Ran Out

Between April 20 and May 7, 1941, the *Pinguin*—disguised as the freighter *Tamerlane*—accounted for three more Allied ships, bringing its total to twenty-eight. But the raider's string was about to run out. A fatally wounded radioman on the flaming tanker *British Emperor* got off a distress signal that pinpointed the German ship's position off the coast of Kenya.

Seaplane pilots dispatched from the British cruiser *Cornwall* flew over the pseudo *Tamerlane* and grew suspicious when the men on deck failed to wave at them. On May 8, the *Cornwall* caught up with the *Pinguin*, and the outgunned impostor began its last battle.

A British lifeboat looks for *Pinguin* survivors who sought safety from sharks in patches of oil.

A boatload of survivors *(left)* pulls alongside the cruiser *Cornwall.*

After a warm wash, rescued German sailors march below decks to receive dry clothing.

Saving Shipwrecked Foes

With all but its bow obliterated, the *Pinguin* sank quickly. More than 550 men perished with the ship, 213 of them prisoners taken from the *Pinguin*'s earlier conquests. Only sixty of the crew and twenty-two prisoners survived, clinging to wreckage in the oil-coated waters until boats from the *Cornwall* picked them up. Among the dead was Captain Krüder, killed when a shell exploded on the bridge.

Because they had often fought under false colors, the survivors among the *Pinguin*'s crew feared they might be dealt with harshly. But the captain of the *Cornwall* ordered that they receive the humane treatment traditionally accorded a seagoing foe.

THREE

A Deadly Game of Hide-and-Seek

dolf Hitler, in a rare moment of introspection, once confided, "On land I am a hero, but at sea I am a coward." Although the Führer was intrigued by submarines and battleships and held his own in technical conversations, he had no sense whatsoever of naval power or how to conduct a war at sea. His experience, his life's bent, was as a soldier. As a result, the Third Reich's navy, more than any other military service, was the creation of its officers—mostly decent, apolitical men, devoted to their calling.

From the start, Admiral Erich Raeder held the Nazis at arm's length. Despite all pressures, he retained the traditional German naval salute and even the chaplain corps; he forbade his officers to engage in party politics; refused to dismiss old and valued Jewish officers—and when *Kristallnacht*, the Night of Broken Glass, erupted in 1938, he forwarded his angry protest, along with those of Karl Dönitz and Günther Lütjens, directly to Hitler. He and his admirals and engineers were the architects of the German navy's new U-boats and surface vessels; and within the overall plan for the war, at least in the early years, naval strategy and tactics came not from Hitler's headquarters but from the naval high command.

In May of 1941, German aspirations at sea were progressing brilliantly. The navy had been vital to the conquest of Norway. German surface raiders were playing havoc with shipping the world over. German U-boats were slashing through British lifelines. In March, the Allies' Atlantic losses had come to 350,000 tons; in April, the losses in all theaters reached an astounding 700,000 tons—unendurable for very long. It seemed to Raeder and his strategists that the war at sea was approaching its climax. The time had come for a decisive blow.

The plan was code-named *Rheinübung* (Rhine Exercise), and it called for a massive pincers attack on enemy sea lanes by the German High Seas Fleet. The assault would be simple—and devastating. The battleships *Scharnhorst* and *Gneisenau* would sortie from Brest on the Atlantic coast of France and drive northward against convoys approaching the British Isles. Meanwhile, the new 50,129-ton superbattleship *Bismarck*, unequaled for its

Gunners on the *Prinz Eugen* maintain battle stations during the heavy cruiser's dash through the English Channel under the noses of the Royal Air Force and the Royal Navy in February 1942. A German officer warned that the mission would result in the "burial of our ships at sea."

thirty-two-knot speed, fifteen-inch guns, and massive armor, would break out of the Baltic, swing around Iceland, and slash down from the north. With the *Bismarck* would be the heavy cruiser *Prinz Eugen*, itself formidable at 18,000 tons and thirty knots with eight 8-inch guns. A fleet of seven oilers and two supply ships would keep the battle groups at sea; submarines would serve as scouts.

The odds on success appeared to be excellent. The British had responded to earlier strikes by the *Scharnhorst* and the *Gneisenau* by assigning battleships to escort their convoys. But no single convoy escort would be a match for the new concentration of German power. And should the Royal Navy mass its battleships to deal with the threat, the Kriegsmarine would still retain the initiative. The convoys would be stripped of heavy protection while the British groped around the Atlantic after the *Bismarck* and its consorts; there was every chance that the battle group could still slip in among the wallowing merchantmen and raise havoc. Moreover, a diversion of British strength to the North Atlantic would have welcome side effects, particularly in the Mediterranean, where the Afrikakorps required seaborne supplies and where the invasion of Crete was about to begin.

For all its promise, Rhine Exercise got off to an inauspicious start. Scarcely had the planning commenced than the Brest dockyard informed Berlin that the *Scharnhorst* would be undergoing an engine refit until June, well past the latest date for the sortie. That left only the *Gneisenau* as the southern claw of the pincers. While Raeder pondered that bit of news, the *Gneisenau*, too, was lost to the operation. On April 6, a lone RAF bomber

swept low over Brest and, before it was shot down in flames, put a torpedo into the *Gneisenau* at its mooring; the explosion ripped a huge gash in the stern, damaging a propeller shaft. This and a later RAF raid knocked the battleship out of action for eight months. Only the *Bismarck* and the *Prinz Eugen* remained to carry out Raeder's grand design.

Raeder and Admiral Lütjens, who was to command the task force, debated whether to postpone the operation. Lütjens argued for a delay until the *Scharnhorst* and *Gneisenau* were ready. Moreover, the new battleship *Tirpitz*, twin to the awesome *Bismarck*, was undergoing sea trials; it would be available in mid-July, and then Rhine Exercise could go forward at even greater strength. But Admiral Raeder refused; the operation must proceed as scheduled. The *Bismarck* would act as a lure, drawing the British battleships away from the convoys and enabling the *Prinz Eugen* to rush in like a wolf among sheep.

The dour, austere Lütjens had grave misgivings. Two ships against the assembled might of the Royal Navy? Fatalism crept into the admiral's thinking. "I realize," he told a colleague, "that in this unequal struggle between ourselves and the British navy, I shall sooner or later have to lose my life." Nevertheless, early in May Lütjens and his staff were piped aboard the *Bismarck* in the port of Gotenhafen. The breakout would come in the dark new-moon period toward the end of the month.

Commanding the *Bismarck* was Captain Ernst Lindemann, forty-five years old and one of the navy's ablest officers. It was fitting that he should captain the *Bismarck*, for he literally lived the motto of Prince Otto von Bismarck: *Patriae inserviendo consumor*—"I am consumed in the service of the fatherland." Lindemann radiated a calm competence, and the men trusted him. The captain of the *Prinz Eugen* was Helmuth Brinkmann, a classmate of Lindemann's at the Mürwik naval academy and also highly respected. Both their ships had all-volunteer, regular navy crews, averaging twenty-one years of age, with little combat experience but honed to the sharpness of a Solingen blade.

On May 5, Hitler arrived in Gotenhafen to inspect the *Bismarck* and its crew. After touring the ship, he held a small reception in the wardroom. When Hitler nervously suggested that the Royal Navy's numerical superiority presented a grave danger, Lütjens responded elliptically by saying that the *Bismarck*'s vast superiority over any single British battleship gave him no apprehensions on that score; presumably he felt that given his ship's speed and maneuverability, he could take on the enemy one at a time. But, he added, torpedoes from carrier-borne British planes would be a menace in any Atlantic operation.

The two warships were ready to sail on the night of May 18, both freshly camouflaged to confuse submarines, with white waves at bow and stern and black-and-white stripes angling across hull and superstructure. Leaving Gotenhafen separately, they steamed steadily across the western Baltic and slipped through the Kattegat, the narrow passage between occupied Denmark and neutral Sweden. Nosing into the North Sea late on May 20, the *Bismarck* and the *Prinz Eugen* joined up at Arkona and swung northward along the Norwegian coast.

All seemed to be going well. No patrolling British submarines were reported; the only aircraft overhead were relays of protective Messerschmitts. But the ships had already been sighted; a Swedish cruiser had spotted them as they transited the Kattegat. The news was swiftly relayed to the British naval attaché in Stockholm by two pro-British officers in Swedish intelligence. Within hours, it was crackling across the airwaves to London. Coast watchers of the Norwegian Resistance also saw the German task force gliding past, and their confirming report was transmitted to London on a clandestine radio set.

When word reached Admiral Sir John Tovey, commander in chief of the Home Fleet, on the *King George V* at Scapa Flow, he immediately ordered the far-flung ships under his command to prepare for action. Within the anchorage, the battle cruiser *Hood*, the aircraft carrier *Victorious*, the new battleship *Prince of Wales*, his own *George V*, and a score of cruisers and destroyers recalled men who were ashore and got up steam. Then Tovey paused to see where the German battle group might be heading.

He did not have long to wait. On the morning of May 21, Admiral Lütjens abruptly turned his task force into the fjord leading to the Norwegian port of Bergen. The move surprised many of his officers. Speed was essential for the getaway, and Bergen was within easy reach of RAF reconnaissance planes flying from Scotland. Nevertheless, Lütjens ordered the *Bismarck* to anchor in Grimstad Fjord, the *Prinz Eugen* in nearby Kalvanes Bay. The admiral was not one to confide his reasoning; perhaps he was waiting for bad weather to mask the final dash northward. The crews were put to work painting over the hulls in battleship gray, a more effective camouflage in the haze of the northern seas. The *Prinz Eugen* also took the occasion to top off its fuel tanks, but the *Bismarck* did not, and this, too, puzzled Lütjens's officers. The first rule for a warship was to fuel at every opportunity, and the *Bismarck* had already burned 1,000 tons coming north. However, a German tanker was only a day's distance away. Lütjens may have planned to rendezvous en route.

That afternoon, while the *Bismarck*'s crewmen continued to paint, a camera-equipped Spitfire flew over at 25,000 feet, too high to be seen or heard. Tovey soon had the answers he needed. The *Bismarck* and a heavy

Admiral Günther Lütjens inspects the crew of the heavy cruiser *Prinz Eugen* in the Baltic Sea harbor of Gotenhafen on May 18, 1941. With Lütjens in command, the *Prinz* and the *Bismarck* sailed that day on a fateful sortie into the Atlantic.

cruiser were in fact in Norwegian waters, obviously poised to break out into the Atlantic. By midnight, the *Hood* and the *Prince of Wales* were steaming out of Scapa Flow, bound for Iceland and the Denmark Strait.

Lütjens and his battle group also were on the move. The weather was bad, with a sharp wind blowing in heavy rain clouds—precisely what Lütjens hoped for. Even if the British had detected his movements up to now, their planes and ships would never be able to track him through the storm. Leaving their destroyer escort behind, the *Bismarck* and the *Prinz Eugen* slipped past Grimstad Fjord's rocky headlands and headed due north to the mist-shrouded wastes of the Norwegian Sea.

The next morning, the weather worsened. "Low, dark rain clouds driven by a steady wind from astern ran with us like sheltering curtains," recalled Baron Burkard von Müllenheim-Rechberg, a young gunnery officer on the *Bismarck*. Visibility was down to barely 400 yards. To maintain formation, the two ships had to turn on their searchlights. "Our passage was truly ghostly," said Müllenheim-Rechberg, "as we slipped at high speed through an unknown, endless, eerie world and left not a trace." It appeared to Lütjens and his officers that they had made a clean escape and would soon be at large in the Atlantic, preying on no fewer than eleven merchant convoys known to be crossing the ocean. The only disquieting signal came from B-Dienst, the navy's radio intercept group; it reported from decoded messages that the British had observed the German battleships and expected them in Arctic waters.

The British made the next move. On May 22, an RAF observation plane, battling clouds and squalls, had flown low over Bergen and radioed a

report: The German vessels were gone. Tovey sallied forth in his flagship, the *King George V,* accompanied by the *Victorious.* The battle cruiser *Repulse* steamed from the Clyde River to rendezvous off the Hebrides. Tovey also signaled the cruisers *Norfolk* and *Suffolk,* which were already patrolling near Iceland, to keep a sharp watch on the narrow Denmark Strait. It was the latter vessels that Lütjens's lookouts spotted as the *Bismarck* and *Prinz Eugen* raced through the strait late on the afternoon of May 23. The weather had cleared, leaving only patchy fog and intermittent snow squalls; a light film of ice covered the sea, causing a bell-like tinkling sound as the ships' bows knifed through the water.

The *Suffolk* was the first to appear, a tiny silhouette trailing astern. A few minutes later, the *Norfolk* loomed out of the fog to port. The *Bismarck*'s guns roared, firing in anger for the first time. Gouts of water 200 feet high bracketed the *Norfolk,* but it escaped into the mist. The British cruisers settled into place fourteen miles astern of Lütjens's battle group, the *Suffolk*'s powerful new radar tracking the *Bismarck* even when the battleship's tall superstructure disappeared from view. The cruisers sent a stream of position reports to London, to Tovey, and, not least, to the *Hood* and the *Prince of Wales,* only 300 miles away and on an intercepting course.

The first shots from the *Bismarck*'s guns had put its forward radar out of action, and Lütjens ordered the *Prinz Eugen* into the lead. "At almost thirty knots we sped through the half-light of the Arctic night," recalled Müllenheim-Rechberg, "dodging into fog banks, rainsqualls, and snow squalls." Finally, at ten o'clock at night, Lütjens ordered the *Bismarck* into a 180-degree turn, hoping to confront and destroy his pursuers. But the British cruisers, alerted by radar, spun away into the gloom. The *Bismarck* resumed its southerly course. The Germans' best hope now was that the enemy's main force had loitered in Scapa Flow until too late to intercept.

Shortly after five o'clock on the morning of May 24, 1941, the hydrophones protruding from the hull of the *Prinz Eugen* picked up sounds of propellers. Two fast-moving ships were approaching on the port bow—and from the sound of the screws, they were heavy vessels. Immediately, every officer on the German cruiser's bridge grabbed binoculars and scanned the eastern horizon. Messages flashed to the ship's radar station, asking if any blips had appeared on the screens; the German radar showed nothing—the enemy was beyond its range.

After a nerve-racking forty-five minutes, one of the *Prinz Eugen*'s gunnery officers saw smoke to the southeast, then the masts of two warships. Instantly the alarm bells went off. Captain Brinkmann materialized on the bridge to take charge, sending an "enemy sighted" signal to the *Bismarck.* The big guns of the two ships swung to port.

Off the coast of Iceland, sailors on the *Prinz Eugen* watch apprehensively as shells from the British battle cruiser *Hood* fall astern, erupting in towers of seawater 250 feet high. The *Prinz Eugen* emerged from the encounter unscathed.

Lieutenant Commander Paul Schmalenbach, the *Prinz Eugen*'s expert on enemy ship silhouettes, announced what no one wanted to hear. The vessel now visible on the left was a large modern one, probably a battleship of the *King George V* class. The one on the right was almost certainly the *Hood*, the British battle cruiser famed around the world. Launched in 1918 and named after a family that had given Britain four admirals, the *Hood* was meant to combine the speed of a cruiser with the firepower of a battleship. It was immense—thirty-two feet longer even than the *Bismarck*, though lighter by 4,000 tons—with a thirty-two knot speed and eight huge fifteen-inch guns capable of hurling a one-ton projectile sixteen miles. Symmetrical and handsomely powerful in appearance, the *Hood* had captured everyone's imagination on a series of goodwill cruises during the 1920s and 1930s. And although the *Hood* was an old vessel now, it was similar to the *Bismarck* in speed and firepower. Only in armor was it lacking; to achieve their compromise, British naval architects had given the *Hood* only three and a half inches of armor on its upper decks. The battle cruiser would be vulnerable to long-range, or plunging, fire.

As Schmalenbach made his identification, one of the far-off warships

Belching smoke and flame, the *Bismarck*'s big guns fire at the *Hood* during their long-range duel in the North Atlantic. After the *Hood* exploded and sank, Fleet Commander Lütjens told the *Bismarck*'s crew, "You have covered yourselves with glory."

loosed a salvo from its main forward turrets. The mighty blasts were an extraordinary sight, even from thirteen miles away; one officer on the *Prinz Eugen* compared them to "great fiery rings like suns." Shortly thereafter, the other distant warship also burst into volcanoes of flame and smoke. "He's fired!" yelled an agitated petty officer on the *Prinz Eugen*'s bridge. "Keep calm, man. Of course he's fired," replied Captain Brinkmann. "Now let's see what comes of it."

With a dozen or so British shells hurtling toward them, the deck officers of the *Bismarck* and the *Prinz Eugen* braced for answering blasts from their own guns. But seconds passed and no order to fire came from Lütjens. Plainly, he did not want to believe his eyes. The latest German intelligence had reported the British Home Fleet still anchored in Scapa Flow, 1,000 miles away. And Lütjens's orders were to go after merchant shipping while avoiding a major engagement with battleships if at all possible.

The shell-timing stopwatches continued their ticking, and the *Bismarck*'s Captain Lindemann was heard to mutter, "I will not let my ship be shot out from under me." At last, Lütjens gave the order, "Permission to fire." Instantly the fifteen-inchers on the *Bismarck* erupted in two quick four-gun salvos. The eight-inchers of the *Prinz Eugen* were only a few seconds behind. Thick, acrid clouds of cordite smoke enveloped the decks and superstructure, choking the men on the bridges and in the gunnery-control lookouts. As the German shells screamed away, the first British salvos rumbled in, hitting the water with earsplitting roars and sending immense geysers into the air. The *Hood*'s shells barely missed the *Prinz Eugen*. Those fired at the *Bismarck* by the other warship—it was the new 35,000-ton *Prince of Wales*—fell 1,000 yards over the mark.

In the *Bismarck*'s fire-control center, Commander Adalbert Schneider, the chief gunnery officer, was getting a salvo every forty seconds from his young turret crews. "Short," he called, marking the first fall of shot. Then, "over." Then, "straddling." Eyes glued to his range finder, Schneider announced coolly, "The enemy is burning." Now he demanded, "Full salvos, good rapid." Two more four-gun salvos hurtled from the *Bismarck*'s fifteen-inchers. "Wow!" cried Schneider. "That really ate into him." Then other voices shouted, "She's blowing up! She's blowing up!"

An eight-inch shell from the *Prinz Eugen* had started a fire on the *Hood*'s boat deck, and the *Bismarck*'s third and fourth salvos destroyed the battle cruiser. Plunging down from a range of 14,100 yards, a one-ton shell punched through the *Hood*'s thin deck armor. It touched off first a four-inch gun magazine, then the two main after magazines; 100 tons of cordite went up in a huge mushrooming column of flame and smoke. The mainmast and part of the after turret could be seen whirling through the air; bits

of ammunition shot skyward and detonated like star shells. As the *Hood* disintegrated, its broken bow rose in the path of the frantically swerving *Prince of Wales;* its stern drifted off a little way before sinking. All but 3 of the 1,419 men on board perished. "Poor devils. Poor devils," murmured the *Prinz Eugen*'s gunnery officer. It was almost exactly 6:00 a.m. Less than eight minutes had passed since the first salvos.

Happy pandemonium engulfed the two German ships. Crewmen pounded one another on the back and yelled and sang. They had sunk the world's most famous warship, the pride of the Royal Navy. Officers had to shout and curse to force their men back on the job. The *Prince of Wales* was still out there—and finding the range; its sixth and seventh salvos straddled the *Bismarck* and scored three hits. Both the *Bismarck* and the *Prinz Eugen* swung their guns to the new target and fired almost simultaneously. Their aim was near perfect. One fifteen-inch shell crashed through the *Prince of Wales*'s bridge, killing everyone except the captain and a signalman. Other shells blasted away the compass platform, a gun director, and the radar station. That was enough. At 6:09 a.m., the *Prince of Wales* laid a smoke screen and sped off to the southeast. Lindemann and Lütjens argued about whether to pursue the enemy; Lindemann wanted to finish off the battle, but Lütjens overruled him. It was time to push on.

In the wardrooms of the German warships, the two gunnery officers were congratulated again and again. There was a special issue of cigarettes and chocolate. The victory was proclaimed a birthday present for Admiral Lütjens, fifty-two years old on the morrow. The naval high command was in a paroxysm of joy, and the news, trumpeted by Joseph Goebbels's Propaganda Ministry, set off celebrations all over Germany.

Yet the *Bismarck*'s awesome triumph represented a setback for Lütjens's strategic plan. His mission had been to escape unseen into the Atlantic, to use his guns to sink merchant ships and help throttle Britain's maritime lifeline. But the task force had been found and attacked even before reaching its operational area. Two British cruisers were still dogging the Germans' wake, tracking Lütjens's every turn. Surely every available ship in the Royal Navy would soon join the hunt. Lütjens's ability to do any commerce raiding—or even to reach port safely—was in jeopardy.

Lütjens's decision whether to continue or run for shelter was made for him. The *Bismarck* was in some difficulty. One of the hits scored by the *Prince of Wales* had holed the port bow, severed a fuel-transfer pipe, and let in 2,000 tons of seawater. The ship's bow was down two or three degrees, and its speed was cut to a maximum of twenty-eight knots. Another shell had struck below the waterline beneath the armored belt and just behind

A motion-picture sequence taken from the stern of the *Prinz Eugen* documents the swift demise of HMS *Hood* seven miles away. At the top, the *Hood*'s magazine explodes in a burst of smoke. In the middle frame, the *Prince of Wales* emerges from the smoke (far right), and a brace of shells from the *Bismarck* create twin spouts of white water as they fall short. At left, the *Norfolk* trails a cloud of black smoke as it charges toward the action. In the bottom frame, the *Norfolk* (left) continues to advance; the *Prince of Wales* has turned away to port, and a thinning cloud of smoke is all that remains of the *Hood*.

the conning tower. It exploded against a bulkhead, caused a flood in a boiler auxiliary room, and ruptured several fuel tanks. The explosion also knocked out some fuel valves; the *Bismarck* was leaving a trail of oil, and worse, was deprived of the use of 1,000 tons of oil in its forward tanks. Lütjens's failure to refuel in Norway was having serious consequences.

Reluctantly, Lütjens decided that the *Bismarck* needed shipyard attention. The *Prinz Eugen*, undamaged and as fast as ever, would head into the mid-Atlantic and do what raiding it could. The *Bismarck* would run on southward, skirting well to the west of Ireland, then turn and head for the coast of France and the ports of Saint-Nazaire or Brest. At 6:14 p.m. on May 24, a code word—aptly, "Hood"—flashed from the *Bismarck*'s signal lamp to the *Prinz Eugen*. The *Bismarck* then engaged the trailing British cruisers long enough for the *Prinz Eugen* to break away to the south.

By late in the evening of May 24, virtually every British warship in the Atlantic was on the chase, guided by reports from the leechlike cruisers *Suffolk* and *Norfolk*. Closest was the *Prince of Wales*, with its sister ship, the *King George V*, 250 miles beyond. The carrier *Victorious* was bucketing along south of Iceland only 120 miles east of the German battleship. To the south was the old but heavily gunned battleship *Rodney*. Most vitally, as it turned out, the Royal Navy's Force H from Gibraltar—including the carrier *Ark Royal* and the battle cruiser *Renown*—had been ordered to speed northwest on the chance of crossing the *Bismarck*'s path.

Soon, Admiral Lütjens and Captain Lindemann had evidence of what they feared most: carrier aircraft. It never grew completely dark in late May at those high latitudes, and now out of the grayness buzzed nine Swordfish torpedo planes—wood-and-canvas biplanes flying at a mere eighty-five miles per hour and so fragile looking that they were dubbed stringbags by their crews. After taking off from the *Victorious*, the pilots had been guided to the target by the *Norfolk*'s radar. The *Bismarck* was etched in flame as its more than fifty guns fired at the intruders. The Swordfish kept boring in—bullets and shells passing clear through their cloth-covered wings. Every plane got off its torpedoes. But only one of the 1,800-pound projectiles hit, killing a crew member and injuring five others. The warhead had struck where the armor was thickest and did no lasting damage.

The enemy aircraft staggered away, all nine of them somehow making it back to the carrier. Lütjens and his officers were glum. The torpedo planes were certain to try again in the morning. It was imperative to shake off those damnable cruisers.

At three o'clock on the morning of May 25, Lütjens ordered the *Bismarck*'s helmsman to turn hard to starboard, away from the pursuit, and

Odyssey of the Bismarck

Departing friendly waters, the *Bismarck* and the *Prinz Eugen* steamed north and west before descending through the Denmark Strait between Greenland and Iceland. On May 24, the two ships did battle with the *Hood* and the *Prince of Wales*, sinking the *Hood*. The *Bismarck*, damaged in the fight, changed course for German-held Saint-Nazaire. The ship temporarily eluded its many pursuers, but on May 26, torpedo planes from the carrier *Ark Royal* scored a hit that jammed the *Bismarck*'s rudder. Now the ship could steam only to the northwest—toward the oncoming enemy. On May 27, two British battleships and two cruisers converged on the crippled *Bismarck* and bombarded it until the captain opened the seacocks, sinking the ship in 15,000 feet of water.

hold there until the ship had made a huge loop and crossed behind the enemy. Magically, the ruse worked. The radarmen on the *Suffolk* were used to losing contact with their quarry for short periods as they zigzagged to avoid possible U-boat attacks. But as time passed, there were no further radar returns. At five o'clock, out went the forlorn message: "Have lost contact with the enemy." The *Bismarck* had escaped.

But then Admiral Lütjens made a cardinal error. His radar room reported receiving British radar emissions, and he mistakenly concluded that the *Suffolk* was still tracking him. Resignedly, he broke radio silence, sending a pair of messages to Berlin describing the efficient British radar, the sinking of the *Hood*, and his own damage. Listening posts in the British Isles picked up the transmissions and passed on the lines of bearing. Within minutes, the *Bismarck*'s apparent position had been worked out aboard the *King George V*. The first computation was incorrect and sent Admiral Tovey's ships in the wrong direction. But a second computation revealed the *Bismarck*'s position unmistakably, and a partially decoded message indicated that the battleship was heading for the Bay of Biscay.

Catching the *Bismarck* was another matter. Tovey was now out of position, and all the Royal Navy's other heavy vessels were too far away to intercept the German battleship. Throughout the day of May 25 and into the night, the *Bismarck* steamed through heavy following seas that flung the ship forward with a sickening, corkscrew motion.

Morale among the men plummeted at noon, when Lütjens spoke to them of the massive British pursuit and the dangers ahead, concluding: "For us seamen, the question now is victory or death." That attitude dismayed Lindemann; an hour later, he delivered his own message to the crew: The

Bismarck would outwit the enemy and reach safety. A crewman remembered how "the men's faces brightened after the captain's address. They had their courage back." The mood lifted further the next morning when an announcement boomed over the ship's loudspeakers: "We have passed three-quarters of Ireland on our way to Saint-Nazaire. Around noon we will be in the U-boats' operational area and within range of German aircraft."

But the exhilaration quickly faded. Just before half past ten, lookouts spotted a large flying boat skulking in the clouds overhead. It was an American-made Catalina, turned over to the Royal Air Force's Coastal Command under the Lend-Lease Act. Taking off early that morning from northern Ireland—with an American flight instructor as copilot—the long-range patrol craft had droned out over the open ocean on the slim chance of spotting the *Bismarck* through the mists and clouds. Against all odds, the plane's crew had managed to do just that. The radio crackled: "One battleship bearing 240 degrees, five miles, course 150 degrees. My position

Shells from the sixteen-inch guns of the *Rodney* erupt in columns of smoke and water as they fall astern of the doomed *Bismarck (right)*. Minutes after this photo was taken, the *Rodney* found the range and began to demolish the German supership.

49.33 north, 21.47 west. Time of origin, 10:30 a.m., May 26." The *Bismarck* had been found again.

About noon, as the *Bismarck* came within range of friendly forces, a wheeled airplane appeared in the distance, also keeping watch. It was a sure sign that a British carrier lay somewhere over the horizon. The *Bismarck*'s lookouts searched the skies for Luftwaffe support; none materialized. At least two U-boats were in the area; both of them, however, were out of torpedoes and critically low on fuel. All that their frustrated skippers could do was watch the action as it unfolded.

Late in the evening, the enemy "stringbags" arrived. The planes were from the *Ark Royal*, which had rushed north from Gibraltar; the carrier was only about 100 miles away, easy range even for the venerable Swordfish. This time there were fifteen attackers; they came in low over the wave tops, flying so slowly that they seemed to be standing still. The *Bismarck*, as one of its crew put it, became a "fire-spitting mountain"; great arcs of tracers glowing red, green, orange, and white reached out for the Swordfish. The larger guns fired into the planes' paths, hoping the shells would create a wall of water and shell splinters. The ship heeled crazily this way and that as Lindemann sought desperately to comb the torpedo tracks. Then, in quick succession, came two sickening thuds as torpedoes slammed into the *Bismarck*'s hull.

Incredibly, as before, all the Swordfish returned to the carrier. They had dealt the *Bismarck* a blow that would turn out to be fatal. The first torpedo had hit amidships, in the belt of heavy armor. It caused some minor flooding but was of no consequence. The second exploded aft, smashing into the rudder compartments and jamming the ship's big twin rudders. The rudders, which had been hard over in an evasive maneuver when the torpedo hit, were locked at twelve degrees to port. The *Bismarck* executed an uncontrolled turn, engaging and driving off the persistent *Suffolk* as it came about. Then the ship slowed. Divers went into the half-flooded stern compartment to repair the jammed machinery, but hundreds of tons of seawater drove them back. Continued flooding caused a slight list to port as Lindemann tried to steer with his propellers, ordering full speed forward from one turbine, full aft from another. Nothing worked. When a diver finally forced his way to the starboard rudder coupling, he found it hopelessly jammed. An officer suggested blasting the rudders free with explosive charges, but the idea was rejected for fear of damaging the triple propellers—which would leave the *Bismarck* utterly helpless. High seas made outboard repairs impossible. The *Bismarck* turned into the northwest wind, wallowing in the waves, and slowed to a crawl.

All hope of reaching France evaporated. "The older men took the news of the jammed rudder as a sentence of death for ship and crew," recalled Müllenheim-Rechberg. One man summed up the thoughts of many: "Today my wife will become a widow," he said, "but she doesn't know it." Captain Lindemann had been considering an award for his gunnery chief Adalbert Schneider ever since Schneider's crews had destroyed the *Hood*. It had better be now. He recommended to Admiral Lütjens that Schneider was worthy of the Knight's Cross of the Iron Cross, and Lütjens radioed Berlin. When Hitler's adjutant brought him the message, the Führer merely nodded his assent. The award had a posthumous air to it.

The British battleships did not attack that night. Tovey was certain from aerial reconnaissance reports that the *Bismarck* was severely damaged, so he waited, merely sending in some destroyers to snipe at the German ship with torpedoes. None of them hit. But by dawn on the morning of May 27, both the *George V* and the *Rodney* were bearing down hard. At 8:47 a.m., from a range of twelve and a half miles, the *Rodney* launched an opening

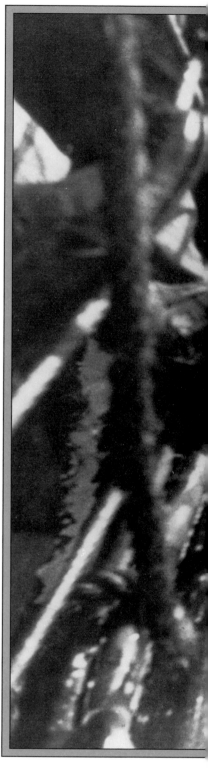

Survivors of the battleship *Bismarck* cling to lifelines lowered from the British cruiser *Dorsetshire*. Hundreds of Germans were left in the frigid water after a reported U-boat sighting prompted the *Dorsetshire* to leave the area.

salvo from its sixteen-inch guns. Less than a minute later, the *George V* fired its fourteen-inchers. Soon the cruisers *Norfolk* and *Dorsetshire*, on the *Bismarck*'s port side, added to the din with their eight-inchers.

The *Bismarck* answered gamely, but the gun crews were exhausted and their aim was off. By nine o'clock, the British ships had found the range. A sixteen-inch shell struck between the forward turrets, knocking both of them out of action. A shell hit the *Bismarck*'s forecastle; another sent a sheet of flame up the superstructure; and still another, from the cruiser *Norfolk*, wrecked the *Bismarck*'s forward fire-control director. The *Rodney*, boldly closing to within four miles, began methodically blasting apart the *Bismarck*'s superstructure, scoring three and four hits per salvo. The back of one turret was destroyed, the flying debris killing men in exposed positions on the bridge. Shells smashed through the armored decks into the engine rooms, and soon the forward half of the ship was burning out of control. When the aft turrets and fire-control station were blasted out of commission, the *Bismarck* was defenseless. Surviving crew members clawed desperately along passages and up ladders. Reaching the top deck, two men ran aft in the drifting smoke, but failed to see a huge shell hole and plunged through into the furnace below. Many of the wounded just sat on the deck, bleeding and waiting for another shell to kill them.

At 10:16 a.m., after forty minutes of point-blank fire, the British called a halt. The *Bismarck* was an inferno, struck by 300 shells or more, a hopeless wreck. But it was still afloat; the thick armor amidships had stood up to the end. One last action remained to be taken. Admiral Lütjens had long since been killed. Captain Lindemann, however, was still alive. He ordered the seacocks opened and the *Bismarck* scuttled. As the ship settled, men in the water saw their captain standing on the forecastle. He raised his hand to his white cap in the cherished navy salute—and as the *Bismarck* rolled over, he and the ship went down together.

The cruiser *Dorsetshire* and the destroyer *Maori* came in to pick up survivors. Hundreds of men were in the water, but only 110 of them had been rescued before a U-boat scare caused the British skippers to depart at full speed. The U-74 later saved another three men while a German trawler saved two more. Those were the only survivors from a crew of 2,206.

The sinking of the *Bismarck* paralyzed the High Seas Fleet. Hitler, furious that this symbol of national pride had been destroyed, ordered Admiral Raeder to risk no more surface ships in the Atlantic. For the moment, the only course open to Raeder was to hold the *Scharnhorst* and the *Gneisenau* at Brest—along with the *Prinz Eugen*, which put in there shortly after leaving the *Bismarck*, its raiding cut short by mechanical problems. With these three powerful vessels lurking in the French port, Raeder could force the British to hold some of their own large warships in home waters. But that was the sole immediate role for his capital ships. "The loss of the *Bismarck*," the admiral said later, "had a decisive effect on the war at sea."

German commerce raiders continued the surface offensive as best they could. Raeder sent out a second wave of small, heavily armed vessels disguised as harmless merchantmen, and enjoyed some success. Five of them—the *Thor*, the *Michel*, the *Stier*, the *Komet*, and the *Togo*—accounted for 263,000 tons of Allied shipping over the course of twenty-two months

Recognition for Service at Sea

On April 10 and 11, 1940, the Royal Navy sank or forced aground ten German destroyers in the narrow fjord leading to the port of Narvik in northern Norway. That June, Admiral Raeder honored the destroyer crews' heroic—if calamitous—resistance by creating the Destroyer War Badge *(bottom right)*, which was awarded to the officers and men of the Narvik squadron.

Raeder later extended eligibility to all destroyer personnel who met certain criteria, such as combat at sea, wounds suffered, or meritorious conduct. The idea caught on, and within a year, the navy authorized the war badges shown here to recognize service on all other classes of surface vessel as well.

High Seas Fleet *(shown enlarged)*

Auxiliary Cruisers

Patrol and Torpedo Boats

Blockade Runners

Minesweepers, Subchasers, and Escorts

Destroyers

before falling prey to various mishaps and a relentless hunt by the Royal Navy. Yet their efforts amounted to no more than a jab at the enemy; only the capital ships could wage a significant surface war. Curiously, it was Hitler, the professed "coward at sea," who ordered the next deployment of Raeder's prized assets.

In the summer of 1941, the Führer became concerned that the British were about to invade Norway and thus turn his northern flank. His renowned intuition told him so. He also sensed that if the increasingly militant United States should enter the war, the Arctic seas would become a vital passage for stepped-up American aid to the Soviet Union. As a counter, Hitler demanded that the High Seas Fleet assemble in the Norwegian fjords: the great *Tirpitz*, the *Bismarck*'s sister ship now fitted out and ready for action; the two remaining pocket battleships *Lützow* and *Admiral Scheer;* the heavy cruiser *Admiral Hipper,* twin to the *Prinz Eugen*—and, of course, the Brest squadron, composed of the *Scharnhorst*, the *Gneisenau*, and the *Prinz Eugen.* All save those at Brest were in their home ports and could easily move north to Norway.

The Luftwaffe could no longer shield the ships at Brest from RAF bombing, and Hitler declared that the fastest, most expedient way for them to withdraw was by dashing north through the English Channel, under the noses of the British. When Raeder and his admirals protested, Hitler coldly replied that if the big ships could be of no use, then they must be scrapped, and their guns and armor sent to reinforce Norwegian coastal defenses.

The planning began forthwith—and, amazingly, the longer Raeder and his staff pondered Hitler's notion, the more feasible it appeared. Deep secrecy was paramount. Until the last minute, only a small group of officers knew what was afoot. Half a dozen code names were invented to cloak the actual one, Operation Cerberus. The ships at Brest were placed under Vice-Admiral Otto Ciliax, one of the Kriegsmarine's most skillful battleship commanders. The Luftwaffe was brought into the scheme, and soon a force of 250 Messerschmitts and Focke-Wulf 190s under General of Fighters Adolf Galland assembled on coastal airfields. They would provide an umbrella against the RAF; air controllers would be on board the ships to direct the fighters. General Wolfgang Martini, the Luftwaffe's director of communications, devised a plan to jam British coastal radar at crucial moments.

The planners also had the daring idea of running the Channel during the day. For one thing, the bold move might take the British by surprise. For another, daylight would be essential for fighter cover and would help the shipboard gunners and shore-based antiaircraft batteries fend off any British attackers. Further, the *Scharnhorst* and its companions, steaming

The auxiliary cruiser *Stier* (left) stands by as its latest victim, the British cargo ship *Dalhousie*, slips stern-first into the Atlantic off Brazil in August 1942. The photo was taken from another German raider, the *Michel*.

at flank speed through the previous night, would make the long first leg of the voyage under cover of darkness. With luck, they might cross the 240 miles from Brest to Cherbourg undetected, then race the remaining 120 miles to the Strait of Dover before the British could fully mobilize. Certainly they would be in home waters before the big British battleships at Scapa Flow had time to steam southward to intercept them.

The date set for the breakout was February 11, 1942, during a new-moon period of dark nights and favorable tides that would add to the ships' speed. That afternoon, the city of Brest was cordoned off so that no one could go into or out of the harbor area while the ships were getting up steam—a move that kept a British agent from reaching his hidden radio set and sending a warning to London. By 9:45 p.m., the ships were under way, steaming out of the harbor, heading for the Cherbourg peninsula at a speed of twenty-seven knots. As expected, the night was dark, with wisps of patchy fog clinging to the sea. Looking aft from the *Scharnhorst*, Admiral Ciliax could make out the dark outline of the *Gneisenau* and behind it the *Prinz Eugen*, both running in perfect line formation. On their flanks were six large destroyers—to be reinforced during the night by more destroyers and by gunboats, minesweepers, and other escort craft putting out from various French ports.

February 12 dawned cold and gray, with mist and scudding rain clouds. The battle fleet had covered 250 miles and, to Admiral Ciliax's relief, seemed to be undiscovered. No British submarines had been detected; the RAF aircraft that normally patrolled the Channel approaches seemed to have missed the long line of swiftly moving vessels. The admiral, hunched in his greatcoat on the *Scharnhorst*'s bridge, drank a cup of steaming coffee while

he waited for Galland's fighters to take position; sixteen fighters would be constantly overhead, and for twenty minutes of each hour as the relays changed, there would be thirty-two defending aircraft. Ciliax feared a trap, but he had come too far to do anything except shrug and race on.

In fact, the British had yet to realize that the German fleet was on the move. The radar jamming had been so cleverly done that British operators along the coast of Kent took it for atmospheric interference. The few blips coming through did not make much sense, and nobody passed on the scattered reports to higher headquarters, where a pattern might have been detected. The first true warning came by accident. At 10:42 a.m., a pair of Spitfires chasing some Messerschmitts over the Channel saw below them the astonishing panorama of Admiral Ciliax's fleet. A few minutes later, two other British aviators, on routine patrol, broke through the clouds to see the same amazing sight. Now at last, in late morning, the defense system began to stir. Orders were telephoned to RAF Coastal Command airfields, to a destroyer flotilla at Dover, to squadrons of torpedo boats, and to coastal artillery batteries. But the reaction was hesitant and piecemeal; as Hitler predicted, the British had been caught by surprise.

Ready first were the Dover coastal batteries, which hurled salvos of nine-inch shells toward the distant, haze-hidden German ships hugging the French coast. The salvos came down a mile short, and after thirty-three useless rounds, the Dover batteries ceased firing. By noon, Ciliax's flotilla had cleared the Channel's narrowest stretch—between Dover and Calais—and slipped from view. The admiral allowed himself the faint hope that he might escape without a fight. His ships had traversed 360 miles of forbidden waters; only 200 more and they would be home.

As the German fleet drove into the narrow sea between Ostend and the southeast corner of England, two gunboats and a squadron of motor torpedo boats (MTBs) came boiling out of Dover harbor, bouncing and slewing at thirty-five knots through a choppy sea. The *Scharnhorst* and its destroyer escorts drove them off with a hurricane of shellfire; the frantically dodging MTBs managed to launch a handful of torpedoes, but none hit.

Almost immediately, the German gunners faced another threat, this one from half a dozen Swordfish torpedo bombers, the same type of aircraft that had done in the *Bismarck*. But there was to be no repeat. Though escorted by ten Spitfires, the Swordfish were easy prey for Galland's Me 109s and FW 190s. The German fighters howled down on the lumbering formation, pumping in machine-gun and 20-mm cannon fire that chewed off wings, exploded fuel tanks, and ripped away long streamers of fabric. Several of the FW 190s dropped their wheels and flaps and throttled back almost to stalling speed in order to stay on the tails of the Swordfish. Meanwhile,

In the German-held harbor at Brest, a gunnery crew on the *Prinz Eugen* drills with a new 20-mm quadruple antiaircraft gun. The weapon had been mounted on the ship's deck early in 1942 to add firepower for the dash up the English Channel.

gunners on the ships fired into the sea to create a defensive curtain of water and shell splinters. One by one, the torpedo planes crashed into the Channel, foundered, and sank. Thirteen of the eighteen airmen aboard died; five wounded survivors were plucked from the water by British boats. Not one of the torpedoes had struck home.

Admiral Ciliax, watching the attacks from the *Scharnhorst*'s bridge, was astonished at how ineffective the British response had been so far. His next serious concern was mines. Both sides had sown the Channel with thousands of the devilish weapons. German minesweepers had worked for days to clear a path through the fields, but in places the safe area was barely half a mile wide—and easy to miss.

As though confirming Ciliax's worst fears, the *Scharnhorst* was suddenly rocked by a heavy explosion. Its engines stopped, and within moments the 38,092-ton warship lay still in the water. A check by the ship's engineers showed that a mine had damaged both the hull and the propellers. Fearful that repairs would take many hours, Ciliax ordered the destroyer Z-29 to come alongside. The Admiral leaped nimbly from the *Scharnhorst* to the smaller ship's heaving deck, and the Z-29, now the Admiral's flagship, surged forward to catch up with the main fleet.

Still the British failed to mount a concerted assault. A couple of squadrons of Beaufort light bombers scrambled into the air, but some had not been armed with torpedoes, and others failed to rendezvous with their fighter escorts. A few of the Beauforts eventually located the main body of German ships but did no harm. Nor did the bombs dropped by a squadron of Lockheed Hudson medium bombers.

By the time of these fruitless attacks, the *Scharnhorst*'s engineers had

effected a temporary repair, and the big battleship was hurrying north once more. The rest of Ciliax's squadron, a bit strung out but still steaming at flank speed, had reached the wide part of the Channel off the Belgian coast. Here the Royal Navy delivered a last desperate attack—by two small flotillas of obsolescent destroyers based at Harwich. All six of the destroyers were at least twenty years old and were normally used only for chasing U-boats and trading shots with German torpedo boats. The destroyers had scarcely cleared the Thames estuary before they came under attack by two flights of Luftwaffe bombers. Shortly after that, they were assaulted by mistake—by twin-engine Hampdens of the RAF Bomber Command. "What's another air force," one crewman grunted, "when the lot's against us already." Miraculously, none of the bombs hit. At 3:17 p.m., the leading destroyer, the *Campbell*, picked up the German ships on radar, range nine and a half miles. The *Campbell* and two of its sisters, the *Vivacious* and the *Worcester*,

Flanked by destroyers and torpedo boats, the battleships *Gneisenau* and *Scharnhorst* (*left*) steam through the English Channel on the afternoon of February 12, 1942. At right, lookouts on the *Prinz Eugen*, the third capital ship in the flotilla, scan the horizon; the flags signal a speed of fifteen knots.

raced in to snap at the huge *Gneisenau*, while the other three turned to attack the *Prinz Eugen*.

The lookouts and fire-control officers on the German warships were surprised to see such pint-size adversaries challenging their gargantuan guns. As the British destroyers turned parallel for their torpedo runs, the *Gneisenau* and its escorts sent broadsides of fire sweeping over the water. Fountains of spray leaped around the *Campbell* and the *Vivacious*, and soon the *Worcester* took a series of heavy hits. At the point-blank range of 3,000 yards, the *Gneisenau* laid three salvos into the destroyer, shattering the *Worcester*'s decking, carrying away part of the bridge, and reducing the engine room to scrap. The *Gneisenau* charged on, leaving the floating hulk to be towed away by a rescue ship. Meanwhile, the other destroyers faded gratefully into banks of fog, lucky to escape annihilation. Another attack had failed to inflict the slightest damage on Admiral Ciliax's fleet.

The aft guns of the *Scharnhorst* loose a salvo at an unseen British destroyer while a pair of Messerschmitts fly overhead during a tense moment in the Great Channel Dash. The German fighters provided cover against Fairey Swordfish torpedo bombers *(inset)*, fabric-covered biplanes that earlier had crippled the *Bismarck*.

Repeatedly, during the late afternoon, RAF bombers roared overhead into walls of flak thrown up by the *Gneisenau* and the *Prinz Eugen*. The weather was turning foul, and soon banks of heavy clouds covered the ships. On the Z-29, Admiral Ciliax decided to transfer his flag again; a small antiaircraft shell had exploded spontaneously, cutting an oil-feed line and reducing the destroyer's speed to twenty-five knots. Another destroyer, the *Hermann Schoemann*, was ordered alongside, but the seas had grown too rough for such a maneuver; instead, Ciliax agilely climbed down a rope ladder into a bouncing cutter. As he was transported to the new flagship, his heart swelled at the sight of the *Scharnhorst* thundering by at a full twenty-five knots. At the *Hermann Schoemann*, the admiral scrambled up another rope ladder, was piped aboard, and briskly ordered the destroyer to full speed.

Ahead lay a last narrow passage between the Frisian Islands. And here, at 7:55 p.m., came a searing white flash and an ear-shattering explosion. The *Gneisenau* had struck a mine and suffered a large gash in its hull near the stern. Damage-control teams quickly patched the hole with a steel collion mat, and the battleship steamed ahead at reduced speed. By the next morning, the *Gneisenau* was off the Elbe River. The anchor chain ran out with a rumble; the captain rang finished with engines; and a huge cheer went up from the weary crew. The *Prinz Eugen* arrived a short time later to another ragged cheer.

The lagging *Scharnhorst*, meanwhile, had slammed into a second mine the evening before, and repair crews had spent three hours working under arc lamps before the captain could signal: "Am capable of proceeding at a maximum speed of twelve knots." Ciliax, who had been circling protectively in the *Schoemann*, broke off and took his modest flagship into Wilhelmshaven. Later that morning, the admiral received his captains in his cabin, took their reports, and hosted a victory celebration. To Berlin, he signaled: "It is my duty to inform you that Operation Cerebrus has been successfully completed." And in a personal message to Raeder he added: "It has been a day that will probably go down as one of the most daring in the naval history of this war."

For all the brilliance of the Great Channel Dash, as it would come to be known, the aftermath was a dismal one. The *Gneisenau* was damaged, and a later bombing attack put it out of the war. Repairs to the *Scharnhorst* required six months, and when it sailed again, an overwhelming British fleet was waiting. Most of Raeder's main fleet, however, made it safely to Norwegian waters. The *Tirpitz*, sailing north in mid-January of 1942, was joined by the *Lützow*, *Scheer*, and *Hipper*, and a dozen destroyers. They

never were called upon to repel a British invasion—Hitler's intuition notwithstanding. Instead, they lurked in the Norwegian fjords, a constant threat with a value of its own.

Late in 1941, the British had begun sending convoys past the North Cape laden with planes, tanks, trucks, and other war matériel for the Soviet Union. In the spring of 1942, the Germans mounted a campaign to choke off this flow of arms, and the world's northernmost seas became a desperate battleground. The weather alone was killing. Forming up off Iceland, groups of freighters and their escorts steamed toward the northern tip of Norway before dipping down into the Barents Sea to the ports of Murmansk and Archangel. The brutal polar winds often reached hurricane force, whipping the seas into seventy-foot combers, and frozen spray built up such a burden of ice that it was a constant battle to keep the smaller ships from capsizing. Still, most of the early convoys completed the 2,500-mile trek without serious loss, hidden by the long dark nights of the Arctic winter. But with the lengthening days of spring, this protection vanished, and soon the torment of the Murmansk Run began.

The first serious effort by the German fleet to destroy a convoy involved the *Tirpitz*, and it almost ended in the sort of disaster that had befallen the *Bismarck*. Under the redoubtable Otto Ciliax, the *Tirpitz* sortied from Trondheim on March 9, 1942, and drove north to intercept convoy PQ12. But an overpowering British force was waiting, and after only two days—on orders from Berlin—the battleship turned tail and scurried back to its sanctuary at flank speed.

The near loss of the *Tirpitz* upset Hitler; he ordered that never again would a capital ship put to sea without proof that no British aircraft carrier was within range. Admiral Raeder, for his part, was outraged. The Luftwaffe had given the fleet no air cover—and not much reconnaissance either. Raeder took the issue to Hitler. Soon a chagrined Reich Marshal Hermann Göring was sending squadrons of He 111, He 115, and Ju 88 bombers to northern Norway, many of them newly adapted to carry torpedoes; by the middle of June, no fewer than 264 combat aircraft were massed at airfields around the North Cape. And a dozen U-boats were prowling Norwegian waters on anticonvoy operations.

The German pilots and submarine crews had already savaged four convoys by the time PQ17 sailed from Iceland in late June. The convoy was large and important: thirty-five merchant ships crammed with $700 million worth of armored vehicles, bombers, and other war matériel. Its guardian fleet was formidable. The close escort consisted of six destroyers and thirteen smaller vessels. Just over the horizon were four cruisers and three more destroyers. And coming north from Scapa Flow to serve as distant

A Fleet of Midgets for Tight Places

The smallest, and among the most useful, vessels in the German navy were a class of midget minesweepers called *Zwerge*, or dwarfs. The pint-size craft were the brainchild of Lieut. Commander Hans Bartels, the maverick skipper of a full-size minesweeper charged with clearing the fjords around Bergen, in occupied Norway, of underwater mines planted by the British.

Bartels wanted small, maneuverable boats whose shallow draft would allow them to pass over a mine without detonating it. Finding none, in 1941 he constructed a dozen dwarfs based on the tear-shaped design of a Norwegian fishing boat. About thirty-five feet long, they carried a crew of six and had a three-foot draft.

When the engines Bartels acquired proved too big to fit the minesweepers' narrow sterns, he solved the problem by placing the engine and propellers in the bow and sharpening the old stern into a bow—in effect, turning the vessel around. The resulting hybrids were hardly handsome, but they kept the channels near Bergen clear for the rest of the war.

A column of miniature German minesweepers parades through Norwegian waters behind their larger flagship. Proud of their vessels' modest size, the crews of the coastal security flotilla displayed a dwarf snaring a mine as their unit insignia *(inset)*.

cover was the bulk of the British Home Fleet, including the carrier *Victorious*, the new 35,000-ton battleship *Duke of York*, the American battleship *Washington*—for the United States was now in the war—two cruisers, and another fourteen destroyers.

Reconnaissance planes and U-boats quickly fixed the convoy's position. From Narvik, Admiral Hubert Schmundt ordered his U-boat pack, the Ice Devils, to the chase. The U-boats approached—only to be depth-bombed by the close escort's swarming destroyers. On July 2, the convoy's anti-aircraft guns beat back an assault by He 111 torpedo bombers, the planes inflicting only minor damage. There was an extraordinary moment when an He 115 floatplane crash-landed just ahead of the convoy and the crew clambered into a yellow dinghy. The British destroyer *Wilton* went after the stranded airmen—shooting to kill, said its captain, "because if we let them get away, they may be back another day and sink the lot of us." But the *Wilton* was thwarted when another He 115 landed amid the shell bursts

Ships of the convoy designated PQ17 assemble off the west coast of Iceland in late June 1942 for the voyage to the Russian port of Archangel. The 2,500-mile passage through hostile waters would require almost two weeks.

In a photo taken from the *Tirpitz*, the *Admiral Scheer* and the *Admiral Hipper* steam with their escorts down a Norwegian fjord on July 5, 1942. The three capital ships had received orders to attack convoy PQ17, but before they could leave the fjord, the mission was canceled.

124

and fearlessly taxied up to the dinghy. The men piled aboard, and the pilot got his plane away through a shower of cannon and machine-gun fire.

By July 4, PQ17 had lost an American Liberty ship and a Russian tanker, but the convoy was still in orderly formation. Most of the crucial cargo, it appeared, would make it to Archangel. That evening, however, an urgent message from the Admiralty in London reached the *Duke of York:* "Secret. Immediate. Owing to threat from surface ships convoy is to disperse and proceed to Russian ports." What was more, the two large covering forces were to reverse course and head west, abandoning the convoy.

The escort commanders were stunned. The order could only mean that the Admiralty had learned that the *Tirpitz* and the rest of the German battle

fleet were at sea and bearing down on the convoy. But did it make sense for the escort to flee and for the convoy to scatter? Dispersal was a standard tactic in the open ocean when a large warship threatened, but it would be suicidal in the restricted seas north of Norway. The convoy commanders could only obey. During the night of July 4 and the early morning hours of July 5, they turned their forces about, leaving PQ17 to its fate.

The order had come directly from Britain's highest-ranking admiral, Sir Dudley Pound, who had become convinced on the basis of some fragmentary evidence that the *Tirpitz* was indeed under way and poised to attack. The Home Fleet was still too far away to intervene, and Pound felt that his cruisers and destroyers would be helpless in the face of the German warships. Rather than risk their destruction, Pound had decided—to the dismay of virtually all his senior advisers—to sacrifice the convoy.

In truth, the *Tirpitz*, *Hipper*, and *Scheer* had been on the move the previous day, but they were merely headed for new anchorages farther up the Norwegian coast. There they sat, paralyzed by Hitler's standing order that no major ship could sail unless there was absolute proof that no British carrier lurked anywhere near. The Germans in Norway were unaware of Pound's order, but by the next morning it was clear that something incredible had happened. Excited reports flooded in from scout planes and then U-boats. PQ17 had scattered during the night. Its escorting destroyers were last seen disappearing over the horizon with the retreating cruisers. The convoy's freighters were wandering across the Barents Sea, stripped of protection except from their own meager armament and the light weapons on the corvettes and trawlers that stayed behind.

The slaughter began at 8:27 a.m. The first victim was a new British freighter, the *Empire Byron*, torpedoed by a U-boat. Next to go down was an American ship, the *Carlton*. Then bombers hit the *Daniel Morgan* and the freighter *Washington*, and U-boats accounted for another American vessel, the *Honomu*. By evening, a German count indicated that no more than seven of PQ17's merchant ships remained afloat. The reality was almost that bad. Seventeen ships eventually reached a protected fjord on the big island of Novaya Zemlya. Several of them tried once more to get to port—only to be savaged again by swarms of Ju 88s and submarines. Eleven of the thirty-five merchantmen that left Iceland made it to the Soviet Union. The losses: 430 tanks, 210 aircraft, 99,316 tons of general cargo. The cost in lives: 153 seamen dead.

Ultimately, the cause of the mauling taken by PQ17 was the overriding fear inspired by one huge battleship that spent virtually the entire battle—indeed, the war—riding at anchor. A German victory at sea had been achieved without the *Tirpitz*, or any other capital ship, firing a shot. ✠

The burning Soviet icebreaker *Alexander Sibiriakov* sinks in the Barents Sea on August 25, 1942, after being attacked by the *Admiral Scheer*. Survivors from the crew *(foreground)* have been rescued by the *Scheer*'s launch.

The Toughest Ship Afloat

Broken nearly off, the *Prinz Eugen*'s stern drags in the sea, churning up an unusual wake.

The heavy cruiser *Prinz Eugen* had earned a reputation for resilience even before it led a flotilla into Norwegian waters in February 1942. In less than a year, the ship had survived the battle that sank the *Bismarck*, endured RAF bombings at Brest, and completed a daring daylight dash up the English Channel. Now Hitler was shifting his sea power northward, and the *Prinz Eugen* would soon have to demonstrate its toughness again.

For three days, rain and snow sheltered the flotilla from attack, but the foul weather and long hours at battle stations exhausted the crew. Because visibility was poor, Admiral Otto Schniewind, the flag officer, ordered the *Prinz* slowed to eighteen knots as it approached Trondheim, Germany's main naval base in central Norway. Four British submarines were lying outside Trondheim Fjord. At dawn on February 23, one of them, the *Trident*, fired its torpedoes at the *Prinz Eugen*. A direct hit nearly severed a huge section of the German cruiser's stern. Although the ship's propellers and turbines remained intact, all twelve boilers blew their safety valves, and the rudder, with the stern structure resting on it, was jammed at ten degrees to port.

The *Prinz* had become a sitting duck, but its luck improved. After two hours, the ship's engineers had steam up again. By running the starboard and center propellers at varying speeds and backing or stopping the port screw, Captain Helmuth Brinkmann got his vessel under way and reasonably on course. Literally dragging its tail behind it, the *Prinz Eugen* limped into the fjord, which became both its haven and its prison.

When an explosion close astern sent up a huge column of water, members of the *Prinz Eugen*'s crew speculated, with relief, that a British torpedo had detonated prematurely. Just at that moment, a second thundering report racked the ship and momentarily left it shuddering in the water.

Compartments beneath the fantail took the brunt of the second torpedo's explosive force; berthed there were scores of sailors and 200 soldiers returning from furloughs in Germany. The soldiers had orders to stay belowdecks in case of action, and some of them were trapped below the waterline. For an hour they could be heard knocking frantically for help. Then the sound dwindled. Miraculously, a search of the vessel revealed only moderate casualties—five dead, twenty-eight wounded.

The *Prinz Eugen* moored at Trondheim in winter darkness. When daylight came, the wounded were carried ashore for treatment, and the dead for burial in a snow-shrouded military cemetery. Two of those who were wounded in the explosion were the flight crew of the *Prinz Eugen*'s floatplane; they had been preparing to go aloft to search for submarines when the *Trident*'s torpedo struck.

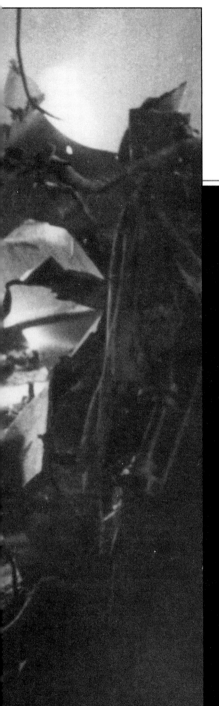

A
Torpedo's
Aftermath

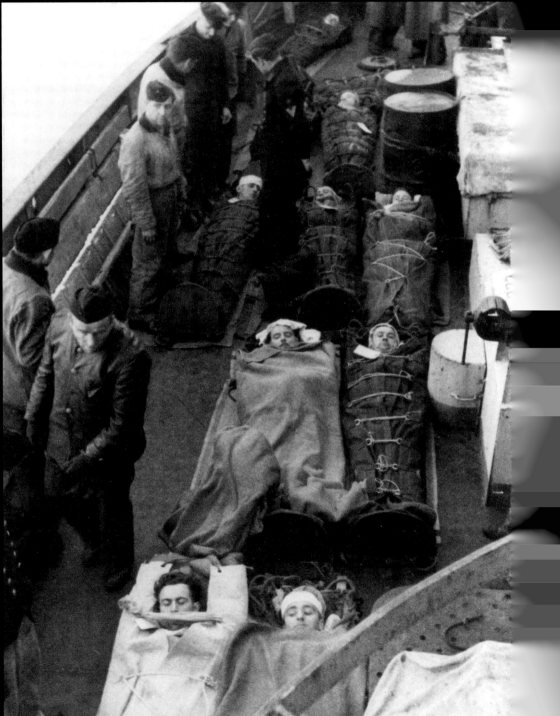

Sunlight streaming into the *Prinz Eugen*'s wrecked stern quarters reveals the force of the explosion. Most of the sailors berthed here were at battle stations when the torpedo hit.

Strapped tightly into basket stretchers, the wounded wait to be taken ashore. More than half of the casualties were soldiers who were returning to occu-

A Stern in Need of Surgery

Launched at the Germania-Werk shipyard in Kiel in 1938 with Hitler and an international array of dignitaries in attendance, the *Prinz Eugen* was named for Prince Eugene of Savoy, an eighteenth-century field marshal of the Austrian Empire. The proud ship displaced 14,800 tons and measured 654 feet from stem to stern. The torpedoing less than four years later lopped forty-five feet off the vessel's length. The blast left the quarterdeck tilted rakishly downward, seemingly held on only by its mooring stanchions.

Amputating the mangled stern and repairing damage to the ship's side and bottom hull plates were difficult tasks that required cutting and welding underwater. To supervise the job, the navy dispatched Erwin Strohbusch, the same expert marine engineer who the previous year had directed the restoration of the *Prinz Eugen*'s main gunnery and damage-control rooms after they were destroyed by British bombs during an air raid on Brest in occupied France.

Looking aft at the *Prinz Eugen*'s nearly submerged fantail, members of the ship's crew contemplate the salvage job that lies ahead of them in an unfriendly

The *Prinz*'s crew relaxes while the ship lies behind a screen of submarine net *(background)*.

Belowdecks in an undamaged portion of the ship, the crew's quarters becomes a crowded maze of sailors' hammocks.

Resisting
Boredom and
the RAF

Shorter, but
Seaworthy
Again

Manpower
to Steer the
Man-of-War

As their officers look on, a team
of sailors test their capacity
to turn the capstan that governs
the ship's new rudders.

The harbor defense boom at
Trondheim opens to let the *Prinz*
slide past under a tow, heading
for a trial run in the fjord.

Sea trials for the jury-rigged *Prinz Eugen* meant pushing the ship to increasingly high speeds while relays of deck hands practiced manhandling the capstan that controlled the newly installed twin rudders. Problems were evident at once. Coughing black smoke, the ship came about much less smartly than before; its turning radius was double what it had been. And at speeds under eighteen knots, it had a tendency to drift sideways.

Confident that British sympathizers among the local population had absorbed all this, Captain Brinkmann took the ship to an estuary known as Beitstad Fjord, far from prying eyes. There he put the *Prinz* through a demanding run; it convinced him that even with manual steering, he could handle the ship at twenty-eight knots.

On May 16, the *Prinz Eugen*, with its escort, slipped through the torpedo nets as though on its way to another day of trials. This time, however, the doughty warship was homeward bound for Kiel. Within hours, along the glacial coast south of Trondheim, it proved itself by threading through the Straits of Oksebaasen, regarded as too narrow for a vessel its size even in the best of circumstances.

The ship became more vulnerable, however, when electric power to the capstan broke down. From that time on, steering would be by manpower alone. And now British planes had the little squadron under continuous surveillance.

The Hard
Run
for Home

Lieut. Commander Paul Schmalenbach, the *Prinz Eugen*'s gunnery officer, shouts orders as
British planes attack off Norway.

Spring's long northern twilight af-
forded the *Prinz Eugen* and its escort ships little cover when the Second Channel Battle, as one German
named it, began on May 17, 1942. A
force of two dozen Blenheims, Hud-
sons, and Beaufighters pounded
the Germans for two hours as they
rounded the coastal curve between
Norway and Denmark. Behind the
bombers came twenty-seven low-
flying torpedo planes.

The German ships fought back
with their own guns and those of
six Messerschmitts that hurried out
to help. In all, the Germans claimed
twenty-two kills, although the British put the toll much lower. Evading bombs and torpedoes with surprisingly rapid turns, the *Prinz* ran
the gauntlet unscathed. The following evening, the ship docked in Kiel,
a survivor once again.

Smoke rises from the muzzles of the *Prinz Eugen*'s 8-inch main batteries.

firing at Royal Air Force bombers beyond the range of the smaller, 4.1-inch guns in the foreground.

Shootout in a Wintry Sea

The 38,000-ton German battleship *Scharnhorst* plows through arctic waters in February 1943. In the frigid winter air, ocean spray froze to the ship's hull, decks, and guns, forming a crust of ice as much as a foot thick.

ubmarine U-354, commanded by Lieutenant Karl-Heinz Herbschleb, was patrolling on the surface in the icy waters above Norway on December 30, 1942, when a sharp-eyed lookout spotted movement along the horizon. Squinting through binoculars into the polar twilight, the sailor made out the dim silhouettes of at least six Allied merchant ships, accompanied by a few small escort vessels, steaming eastward toward Murmansk. Herbschleb fixed their location at fifty miles south of Bear Island and radioed the news to naval headquarters in Berlin.

Admiral Erich Raeder received the report with undisguised delight. Here at last was a chance for the surface fleet to erase the bitter aftertaste left from one of the Kriegsmarine's most successful operations—the smashing six months earlier of convoy PQ17. In that endeavor, fear of meeting the battleship *Tirpitz*, the pocket battleship *Admiral Scheer*, and the heavy cruiser *Admiral Hipper* had caused the British to disperse the convoy, leading to the loss of two-thirds of its ships. But the big German warships did not get a chance to join in the easy pickings. In accordance with Hitler's order that the surface fleet avoid all unnecessary risks, Raeder had left the killing to the Luftwaffe and the U-boats. "They should have let us make *one* little attack," complained Commander Hans-Jürgen Reinicke, first operations officer on the *Hipper*. "Heaven knows, they could always have recalled us after we had bagged three or four of the merchantmen. One should not forget the psychological effect on officers and men."

German destroyer crews also felt cheated. One indignant officer called the big ships "birds of ill omen" to which the destroyers were bound with iron chains. "The mood," he lamented, "is bitter. Soon one will feel ashamed to be on the active list if one has to go on watching other parts of the armed forces fighting, while we, the core of the fleet, just sit in harbor." Now, however, it seemed that the surface fleet would be amply compensated for its long months of idleness.

Upon receiving the U-354's report, Raeder ordered the launching of Operation *Regenbogen*, or Rainbow, a strike plan he had drawn up a few weeks earlier when it became clear that the Allies were about to resume

shipments of supplies to the Red Army through northern Soviet ports. The navy commander in chief instructed Vice-Admiral Theodor Krancke, his representative at *Wolfsschanze* (Wolf's Lair), Hitler's headquarters in East Prussia, to inform the Führer.

At six o'clock that evening, in Alta Fjord, high on Norway's jagged 1,000-mile-long coast, Vice-Admiral Oskar Kummetz, commander of German cruisers, put to sea aboard the *Hipper*. Accompanied by the pocket battleship *Lützow* and six destroyers, Kummetz headed for the Barents Sea. Included in his orders was the warning: "Avoid a superior force, otherwise destroy the enemy according to the tactical situation." Kummetz was not yet clear of the fjord when he received a second caveat from Raeder's chief of staff, Admiral Kurt Fricke: "Exercise discretion in face of enemy of equal

The *Lützow*, a major participant in Operation Rainbow, the ill-fated attempt to intercept an Allied convoy in the Barents Sea, was launched in 1931 as the *Deutschland*, the first pocket battleship. Hitler ordered the name changed because he did not want to risk the sinking of a ship named for Germany.

strength owing undesirability of submitting cruisers to major risk." Fricke's intention was only to emphasize the Führer's well-known phobia about losing a capital ship, but the warning would have a profound effect on the action about to unfold.

Kummetz's would-be prey was convoy JW51B. (The British had recently adopted the code letters JW, instead of PQ, for their convoys, with numbers starting at 51 instead of 1.) Three days before Christmas, JW51B had left Scotland's Loch Ewe with fourteen merchant ships, six destroyers, and five smaller escorts. One of the destroyers suffered compass failure early on and lost contact, but it managed to get home safely on its own. On the fifth day at sea, a gale separated five of the merchantmen and an escort trawler from the other ships. A minesweeper was detailed to search for the missing merchantmen, three of which soon rejoined the convoy unassisted. Of the remaining two, one sailed on alone; the other met up with the lost trawler, and they continued on together. The minesweeper never rejoined the convoy.

The sixteen ships in JW51B's sister convoy, JW51A, had enjoyed better luck. They had sailed a week earlier and reached Murmansk undetected on Christmas Day with 100,000 tons of precious supplies in their holds. (Ironically, five of the ships struck mines after they had reached the supposedly safe harbor.)

Kummetz's plan was to circle north with the *Hipper* and three destroyers, then intercept the second convoy and drive it south, into the guns of the *Lützow* and the other three destroyers. If ever a maritime adventure looked promising, it was Operation Rainbow. The Germans would enjoy a huge advantage in speed and firepower. The *Hipper*'s eight 8-inch guns had a maximum range of more than twenty miles, nearly twice the range of the 4.7- and 4-inch guns on the British destroyers. Moreover, with a top speed of thirty-two knots, the *Hipper* could travel more than three times faster than the convoy. The *Lützow*—originally christened the *Deutschland*—could make twenty-eight knots and carried six 11-inch guns, each with a range of twenty-six miles. Even the German destroyers outgunned their Royal Navy adversaries.

But the weather presented problems, as it always did in the polar winter. Daylight was limited to a few hours each day; and floating icebergs, frequent snow squalls, mist, and fog made navigation hazardous. Slashing waves whipped by sudden gales covered foredecks and bridges with ice, adding hundreds of tons to a ship's weight. Worse, the guns, especially the smaller ones, might freeze solid, and ice on radio antennae and signal lights could hamper communications. Still, that night, Kummetz sent Raeder an optimistic report: "By dawn we should have closed with the enemy."

On the morning of December 31, the first British ships to sight the leading German destroyers mistook them for Soviet escorts steaming out to accompany them to port. Shortly afterward, at a quarter past nine, the destroyer *Friedrich Eckoldt*, ranging ahead of the *Hipper*, opened fire, and the Battle of the Barents Sea began. Lieutenant Herbschleb on the U-354, which was bobbing in heavy seas several miles away, glimpsed the ensuing flashes from the guns and radioed a coded message to Berlin: "Observation of scene suggests battle has reached climax. I see only red." At the headquarters of the naval high command, Admiral Raeder took the U-boat's cryptic message to mean that Kummetz had begun the destruction of the convoy. He passed the information along to Krancke, who in turn told a delighted Adolf Hitler.

The year 1942 had begun auspiciously for Hitler's Germany, but it was ending with a string of disasters: The summer campaign to capture the oil fields of the Caucasus, and with them enough fuel to supply the overextended Wehrmacht, had failed. In November, an Anglo-American army had landed in North Africa, and Erwin Rommel's proud Afrikakorps, which as late as September was within striking distance of Cairo, was defeated at El Alamein. Finally, there loomed the most chilling catastrophe of all—the impending collapse of the German Sixth Army at Stalingrad. Scarcely a week earlier, the last hope of relieving the beleaguered troops had evaporated, dooming nearly 200,000 of them. Now it seemed that the Führer's much-maligned surface navy was about to present him with some sorely needed good news.

At his New Year's Eve party that evening, Hitler confided to his Minister of Foreign Affairs, Joachim von Ribbentrop, and to the SS chieftain, Heinrich Himmler, that a convoy to Murmansk had been sunk in the vacant seas above Norway. He was only awaiting details of the great victory, which he would announce to the world the next day. As the Führer circulated nervously among his guests, however, no further word arrived. More than once he asked, "Krancke, when shall I get my report?" By midnight, Raeder's embarrassed representative could only wring his hands and blame the silence on the shakiness of communications at sea during an arctic winter. Throughout the night, Hitler paced the building, unable to sleep.

Although the official report on the battle would not arrive for many hours, the action had long since ended. In three hours of confused fighting, in visibility so poor that both sides had trouble distinguishing friend from foe, the German navy had suffered a humiliating defeat.

After receiving the *Friedrich Eckoldt*'s fire, the commander of the British escort, Captain R. St. V. Sherbrooke, on board the destroyer *Onslow*, waited

A Trap That Failed

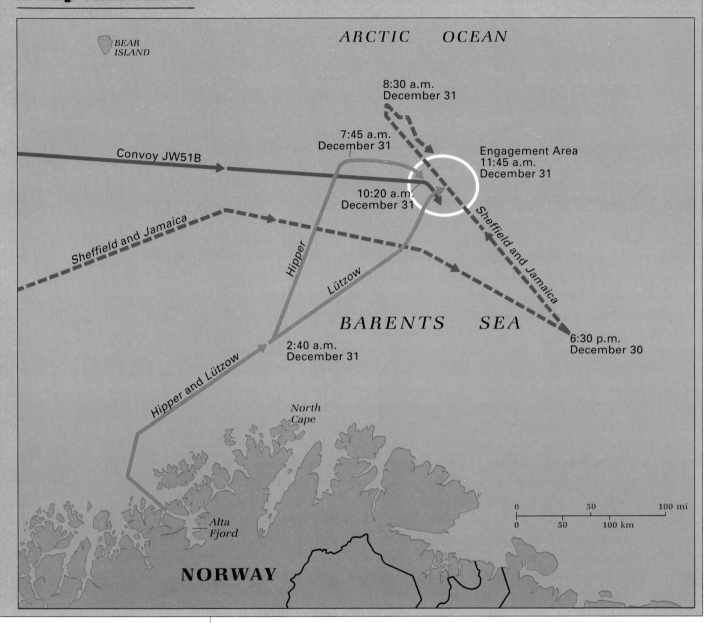

BEAR ISLAND

ARCTIC OCEAN

8:30 a.m.
December 31

7:45 a.m.
December 31

Engagement Area
11:45 a.m.
December 31

Convoy JW51B

10:20 a.m.
December 31

Sheffield and Jamaica

Sheffield and Jamaica

Hipper

Lützow

BARENTS SEA

6:30 p.m.
December 30

Hipper and Lützow

2:40 a.m.
December 31

North Cape

0   50   100 mi
0   50   100 km

Alta Fjord

NORWAY

twenty-six minutes before breaking radio silence. Then he called for help from the light cruisers *Sheffield* and *Jamaica*, which were steaming west from Russian waters to rendezvous with the convoy.

The British destroyers swiftly went into action, laying a smoke screen to give the convoy a chance to make a run for it. Like terriers confronting a giant mastiff, two of the destroyers began a series of feints at the *Hipper*, as if to deliver torpedo attacks. Their boldness paid off. The *Hipper* turned away from the convoy. Shells from the German heavy cruiser sent mountains of water spouting from the iron-gray seas as the destroyers swerved this way and that, steering toward the patch of water last hit, figuring that the *Hipper* would change the range of its guns after each miss.

Inevitably, a salvo struck the *Onslow*, splitting its funnel in two, holing its engine room, knocking out two of its guns, and killing or wounding forty men. Sherbrooke was bleeding heavily and was blinded in one eye. He passed command of the escort to the captain of the destroyer *Obedient*. In

147

the poor visibility, Admiral Kummetz was still unsure how strong an enemy he was up against and did not dare press the attack. But he had succeeded in driving the Allied convoy southward toward Captain Rudolf Stänge of the *Lützow*, as the German plan called for.

At 10:45 a.m., the convoy appeared to Stänge's port as a series of wavering silhouettes. But as the freighters slowly bucked southward, crossing the *Lützow*'s recent wake *(see map, page 147)*, Stänge continued northeastward. Although no British destroyers were nearby, he could not see well enough to attack. In vain Kummetz urged him to pursue the unprotected merchantmen. At about half past eleven, the *Hipper* severely damaged the British destroyer *Achates* and sent another message to Stänge: "Engaging security forces. No cruisers with convoy." Barely a minute later, two shells struck the water near the *Hipper*, sending icy spray flying over the bridge. The shells were larger than any a British destroyer carried—and they came, bewilderingly, from the north. The cruisers *Sheffield* and *Jamaica* had caught up with the battle. More than two hours had elapsed since the start of Kummetz's attack.

Steaming to aid the *Hipper*, Captain Alfred Schemmel in the destroyer *Friedrich Eckoldt* was surprised by shellfire tearing up the water around his ship. He desperately signaled Kummetz: "You are firing at me!" Instantly came the reply: "No. It's a British cruiser." By then it was too late. Struck repeatedly by shells from the *Sheffield* and the *Jamaica*, the *Friedrich Eckoldt* split apart and sank with all 340 hands.

Charging through the heavy seas toward the *Hipper*, the two British light cruisers then subjected the German flagship to almost seventy rounds of fire per minute. The *Hipper* was hit four times in rapid succession. One blast flooded an engine room, cutting the ship's top speed to twenty-eight knots. When Kummetz turned to fight, the smaller British ships dodged nimbly out of range.

Meanwhile, Stänge on the *Lützow* plowed fruitlessly through the polar gloom. Emerging from a snow squall, the ship finally sighted the convoy and began shelling it. Then the British cruisers came in view, and Stänge switched his fire to them.

Even now, despite the arrival of the British reinforcements and the loss of the *Friedrich Eckoldt*, the odds still favored Kummetz. Two light cruisers were no match for a German pocket battleship and a heavy cruiser screened by destroyers. Instead of attacking, however, Kummetz recalled his ships. Inhibited by his orders to avoid confrontation with an equal force, he elected to retreat. With the British cruisers shadowing at a respectful distance, the Germans returned to the safety of Alta Fjord, and Operation Rainbow ended.

The German destroyer *Friedrich Eckoldt* steams along the northern coast of occupied Norway. On December 31, 1942, the ship went down with all hands, a casualty of the Battle of the Barents Sea.

Actual German losses had been slight—the *Hipper* had suffered minor damage and one destroyer had been sunk; the Royal Navy had lost one destroyer and a minesweeper. But the harm done to the Kriegsmarine's fragile morale and shaky reputation was irreparable. It was unthinkable that two big fighting ships and six oversize destroyers could be held off by a handful of destroyers, then driven away by two light cruisers. The Kriegsmarine's failure to destroy a convoy loaded with vital war matériel at this critical point in the war called into question the very existence of the surface fleet.

Kummetz prudently maintained radio silence until he was inside Norwegian waters early on New Year's Day. Through an unlucky coincidence, the landwires in northern Norway had broken down, and, as a result, when Hitler was briefed that day there was still no word from the Barents Sea.

What the progressively more agitated Führer heard instead was a British broadcast claiming that Royal Navy destroyers had stood off a German pocket battleship and a heavy cruiser in arctic waters, damaging the cruiser and sinking a destroyer.

When word of Kummetz's withdrawal at last reached the Wolf's Lair, Hitler flew into a wild rage. He accused the navy of withholding information and refused to listen to any of Krancke's explanations. Screaming for Admiral Raeder to report in person, he declared that he would immediately scrap every big ship in the surface navy and banish the crews and guns to fight ashore. To emphasize his intractability on that point, he ordered it logged into the official war diary.

Raeder put off seeing Hitler until January 6 so that he could gather the facts about Operation Rainbow and, he hoped, allow Hitler time to calm down. But the Führer's anger had not cooled. For ninety minutes, in the presence of Field Marshal Wilhelm Keitel, chief of the High Command of the Armed Forces, and two stenographers, Hitler gave the sixty-six-year-old grand admiral a frightful tongue-lashing. With the exception of the U-boats, the Führer declared, the German navy had been nothing but a failure from its inception. The heavy ships, in which he once had shown lively interest, he now damned as utterly worthless. "He even attacked the spirit and morale of the navy, which, up to then, he had always praised," the stunned Raeder later recalled. "It was glaringly obvious that this

Grand Admiral Karl Dönitz *(right)*, Raeder's successor as commander in chief of the German navy, inspects a destroyer crew in 1943. Dönitz's competence made a favorable impression on Hitler, who gave him a relatively free hand.

whole diatribe was intended for only one thing—to insult me personally."

When Hitler concluded his remarks, Raeder asked permission to speak to him privately. After the others had left the room, Raeder tendered his resignation. He had done so twice before, in the 1930s, and both times Hitler had refused it. This time, after a few words of appreciation for past services, Hitler accepted. To smooth appearances and allay public concern, the official date was put off until January 30, 1943—the tenth anniversary of Hitler's assumption of power and a logical time for the admiral to step aside and accept the strictly honorary post of inspector general of the navy. Hitler asked Raeder to prepare a memorandum detailing his views on the future of Germany's capital ships, and Raeder used the opportunity to make an impassioned plea for saving them. He described the tactical and logistical value of a substantial surface fleet, whose very existence was a defense against attack. He reminded Hitler of Plan Z, agreed upon only four years earlier and then abridged. Raeder asserted that scrapping the big ships would be greeted with joy in enemy capitals, especially London. "England," he concluded, "whose whole war effort stands or falls on the control of its sea communications, would regard the war as good as won if Germany scraps its ships."

Hitler asked Raeder to suggest a successor. Raeder offered two names, a surface-fleet officer, Admiral Rolf Carls, commander in chief of Naval Group North, who was his first choice, and Admiral Karl Dönitz, commander of the U-boat fleet. The Führer chose the latter.

Karl Dönitz was convinced that the only way Germany could regain the initiative was to produce more and better undersea boats to choke off the ever-widening flow of supplies from America. His first priority as commander in chief of the navy was to hasten the building of new U-boats, especially the improved electric boats that could cruise underwater for vastly longer periods of time. Hitler, who had always admired the submarine service, agreed. But Dönitz had no intention of giving up the big ships. Unlike Raeder, he was a tenacious and skillful negotiator. Eventually he convinced the Führer, as Raeder had tried to do in his memorandum, that simply to cut up the surface fleet and place its guns ashore would be both a military mistake and a waste of dockyard time.

Instead, Dönitz proposed to decommission the *Hipper* and the light cruisers *Köln* and *Leipzig*, to leave the damaged *Gneisenau* unrepaired, and to transfer the *Admiral Scheer*, the *Lützow*, and the cruisers *Prinz Eugen* and *Emden* to the Baltic as training ships. Some of the crews could—as Hitler wished—be turned into cannon fodder for the army. But the battleships *Scharnhorst* (presently in the Baltic) and *Tirpitz* should remain in Norway to tie down the British Home Fleet. The moment would

come, Dönitz argued, when those two ships would inflict great losses on the enemy. This, of course, had been Raeder's longstanding position. Dönitz also won from Hitler the concession that in future sea battles, the captains of the major ships would be free to fight as the tactical situation demanded—and not have to wait for approval from a distant headquarters. Hitler liked Dönitz's aggressive spirit; nevertheless his agreement was grudging. Eventually, he predicted, "you will come back to me and admit that I was right."

Nearly a year passed before the surface fleet got its next chance for glory. In March of 1943, the *Scharnhorst* moved up to Narvik, and then, along with the *Tirpitz* and the pocket battleship *Lützow*, to Alta Fjord. There they lay at anchor, surrounded by torpedo nets. The months went by. While the German ships were, in Hitler's pungent words, uselessly "lying around in Norwegian fjords," they kept a good portion of the British navy from being used elsewhere. During the summer, Allied convoys stopped making the Scotland-to-Murmansk run because the German ships were known to be nearby and the long hours of daylight made the convoys especially vulnerable. It was safer and more effective to shift the escort destroyers to the Atlantic, where the U-boat war had intensified again. But with winter coming on, the convoys resumed, and with them came the opportunity Dönitz had foreseen.

The word to sail reached the *Scharnhorst* on Christmas Day, 1943. Despite months of inactivity, the crew's morale had remained high. When the gunnery officer mustered his men on deck to inform them of their mission, cheers drowned out his voice. This, at last, was to be the Operation *Ostfront*, or East Front, that Dönitz had promised Hitler.

The target was the Murmansk-bound convoy JW55B, consisting of nineteen freighters and a large destroyer escort. The convoy was expected to pass 150 miles above the North Cape on the following day, when the forecast called for gale-force winds. Heavy seas would hinder the British warships as they tried to link up with their charges, and they would slow down the *Scharnhorst*'s destroyer escort as well. Snow squalls also were expected, so there would be no aerial reconnaissance—even if the Luftwaffe's Northern Waters Headquarters at Narvik succeeded in getting Göring's approval for the flights.

Several high-ranking officers voiced concern that the primary condition for committing a capital ship—adequate knowledge of the enemy's position—was unfulfilled. The deputy commander at Narvik went so far as to contact Admiral Otto Schniewind, 1,000 miles away at Naval Group North headquarters in Kiel, urging that the operation be deferred. Schniewind

relayed the message to the naval command in Berlin, adding his own concerns. But Dönitz would hear none of it.

The *Scharnhorst* was ordered to embark at 5:00 p.m. The tight schedule allowed for barely three hours to shake off the torpedo nets and get up steam. Orders for the five accompanying destroyers did not arrive until 4:37 p.m., just twenty-three minutes before the scheduled departure. Not surprisingly, Operation East Front was two hours late getting under way.

The *Scharnhorst* had a new skipper, Captain Fritz Julius Hintze, and an inexperienced task force commander, Admiral Erich Bey. Although Bey had made a reputation in destroyer actions at Narvik and in the English Channel, he had never commanded a battleship group before. And, owing to holiday leaves, the *Scharnhorst* would be undermanned.

After Bey had sailed, Admiral Schniewind again communicated with Dönitz to urge that the mission be canceled. At the least, he argued, the destroyers should be withdrawn. Hours passed with no word. At two minutes after midnight on December 26, Dönitz wired back. If the destroyers could not function effectively, the *Scharnhorst* should proceed alone, as an "armed raider." Like Hitler a year earlier, Dönitz was desperate for a dramatic success. He had sold the Führer on the idea that the High Seas Fleet could produce results, if only its captains were not constrained by orders to be cautious. In another message, he commanded Bey to "make bold and skillful use" of the tactical situation. "The fight," he said, "is not to be half finished."

Admiral Bey himself was sufficiently troubled by the weather to break radio silence. He signaled Narvik: "Use of destroyer weapons gravely impaired." His message was as close as an honorable captain could come to a cry for help. But using the airwaves only worsened his predicament. The Royal Navy's listening service picked up the transmission and concluded that a major German ship was at sea. Word was flashed to the heavy cruiser *Norfolk* and the light cruisers *Sheffield* and *Belfast*. It also reached Admiral Bruce Fraser's Home Fleet task force for Murmansk convoys, consisting of the battleship *Duke of York*, the light cruiser *Jamaica*, and four destroyers.

When the alert came, the *Norfolk's* cruiser group was 150 miles east of JW55B, shepherding an empty convoy home from Murmansk. All three cruisers immediately put on speed. Fraser's task force was 220 miles to the southwest. He ordered convoy JW55B to turn northeast and called up four more destroyers. Then he headed the *Jamaica* and the *Duke of York* for the North Cape, hoping to cut off the German ships from their base in Norway.

The *Scharnhorst* possessed heavy deck armor, nine 11-inch guns in three turrets, and a formidable top speed of thirty-one knots. The British light

cruisers were not likely to prove decisive assailants. But the *Duke of York,* a new battleship with fourteen-inch guns, was something else again. Oblivious to any of these threats, the *Scharnhorst* continued northward. The ship was sailing in the blind. To keep from revealing his position, Bey had turned off the surface search radar. At 7:55 a.m. on December 26, not finding convoy JW55B where he had expected it, Bey ordered his five destroyers to fan out to the southwest over a twenty-mile front and some ten miles ahead. He was searching intently for the convoy, when suddenly, at 9:24 a.m., a flare lit the sky. Six minutes later, eight-inch shells began churning the seas around him. Racing westward, the *Belfast* had picked up the *Scharnhorst* on radar from seventeen miles away and had been tracking the battleship for forty minutes. Soon the *Norfolk* and the *Sheffield* also were within range. It was the *Norfolk* that opened fire.

On the *Scharnhorst's* bridge, Captain Hintze hardly had time to switch on his radar when a tremendous explosion racked the foremast, destroying the forward radar aerial and leaving only the aft radar working. Almost immediately, Bey ordered the battleship to turn away from the British cruisers and search for the convoy. Dönitz would later say that Bey should first have put the cruisers out of action with his eleven-inch guns. But Bey's orders were to destroy the merchant ships, and he might have reached them had Admiral Fraser not sent the convoy north to lure the *Scharnhorst* farther from home.

In a kind of nautical blindman's buff played out in heaving seas, the British and German ships blundered through snow, fog, and darkness. For more than two hours after the first guns fired, Bey's destroyers could locate neither the convoy nor their own battleship. Bey and Hintze knew the whereabouts of the three British cruisers. However, when they came within range again, shortly after noon, the cruisers had inserted themselves between the *Scharnhorst* and the convoy. In exchanges of fire, the *Norfolk* was badly hit twice, but Admiral Bey, fearing torpedo attacks, soon turned the *Scharnhorst* away, breaking off the hunt. He had sought the convoy too long. Now he drove south, signaling his misplaced destroyers to return to base.

Bey almost made it home. But at 4:17 that afternoon, piling along at thirty-one knots, the *Scharnhorst* appeared as a faint blip on the search radar of the oncoming *Duke of York.* The range was twenty-two miles. Thirty-seven minutes later, star shells from the *Belfast* sprayed the sky over the *Scharnhorst.* The *Duke of York,* now less than fourteen miles away, began firing. Soon the two great ships were engaged in a running duel. Shells hit the *Duke of York's* masts. They failed to explode, but did cut the aerial gunnery radar. A brave junior officer climbed the mast in freezing

cold and dark to repair it. In the meantime, the *Scharnhorst*, with a four-knot edge in speed, began to pull away.

The *Scharnhorst*'s two forward turrets had been knocked out of action. Another shell damaged a boiler room just above the waterline, severing a vital steampipe to the turbines. The battleship's speed fell to ten knots. The chief engineer patched up the damage, but now the British destroyers were catching up. At 6:24 p.m., Bey and Hintze sent a dramatic message to Dönitz and Adolf Hitler: "We shall fight to the last shell." This was no theatrical boast. The crew transferred massive eleven-inch shells by hand from the ruined forward turrets to the aft turret and kept up a galling fire from the smaller guns still in service.

Dashing in, four British destroyers launched torpedoes, crippling the *Scharnhorst* for good. As the destroyers withdrew, the *Duke of York* and the three British cruisers came on. Their quarry was on fire. Still shooting, the *Scharnhorst* lurched southward. At 7:12 p.m., the *Belfast* knocked out the German ship's last big turret, leaving it with only two 5.9-inch guns. By now, the *Scharnhorst* was dead in the water and listing heavily. Forty-five minutes later, it abruptly turned on end and sank, bow first. Its triple screws were still turning as it slipped beneath the surface. The battleship had taken a frightful pounding—absorbing hundreds of rounds of shellfire and fifty-five torpedo attacks, including at least eleven direct hits.

The *Scharnhorst* went down with 1,968 men on board. Hundreds of them jumped into the sea and tried to swim to the few available life rafts. But the water was only a few degrees above freezing, and within minutes most of them lost consciousness and drowned. Nosing about in the darkness, the British destroyer *Scorpion* scooped up only thirty-six survivors.

The courage of the German sailors had deeply moved Fraser. "Gentlemen," he told his officers that evening, "I hope that any of you who are ever called upon to lead a ship into action against an opponent many times superior will command your ship as gallantly as the *Scharnhorst* was commanded." A few days later, on its way back to Britain, the *Duke of York* sailed over the spot where the *Scharnhorst* had gone down. Admiral Fraser, the British battleship's officers, and a guard of honor stood at attention along the rail as a wreath was dropped into the sea. The fight proved to be the last old-fashioned surface engagement in which the Germans would take part. With the exception of a few Pacific battles, every subsequent confrontation at sea would involve aircraft or submarines.

The demise of the *Scharnhorst* left the German navy with a single battleship, the 50,000-ton *Tirpitz*—soon known as the Lonely Queen of the North. Had the *Tirpitz* gone forth with the *Scharnhorst* at Christmas of 1943, there is no telling what carnage they might have inflicted on convoy JW55B. Even lying in a Norwegian fjord, the *Tirpitz*, with its eight 15-inch guns and forty smaller-caliber weapons, remained a formidable foe. It had almost thirteen inches of steel on its flanks, and steel decks nearly four inches thick. By a supreme irony, this potent engine of destruction had been in action only twice. The first time was a quick slap at convoy PQ12 on March 6, 1942. The second involved a brief run against Allied weather and radar stations in the Spitsbergen archipelago off northern Norway in September 1943. In a single day at sea, the *Tirpitz* and its accompanying destroyers consumed 8,100 tons of fuel. Given Germany's chronic fuel shortage and Hitler's fear of losing a capital ship, there was little chance of its leaving port. But the British did not know that; for years, they watched the *Tirpitz* with a mixture of fascination and fear, like peasants in a fairy tale warily eying a drowsing dragon. So great was the battleship's threat that the Royal Navy held back ships and planes in the Home Fleet that were badly needed elsewhere. In December 1941, out of fear of the *Tirpitz*, the aircraft carrier *Victorious* was kept at home, and the battleships *Prince of Wales* and *Repulse* sailed to Malaysia unprotected. Japanese dive bombers sank them both.

Between January 1942 and November 1944, the British tried all manner of ways to destroy the dreadnought, attacking it on thirteen occasions from the air alone. The first and most daring surface raid came in late October of 1942, when Hitler's drive toward the Caucasus was in high gear and the pressure on the western Allies to get supplies through to the Russians was tremendous. At the time, the *Tirpitz* was anchored in Trondheim Fjord, nearly 100 miles inland.

The British had secretly converted a fishing trawler to carry six frogmen and two torpedoes, called Chariots. When the trawler reached Norwegian waters, the Chariots were slipped into the sea and attached to wires with special fittings so they could be towed underwater. The trawler's regular crew of Norwegian fishermen bluffed past the German guards at the entrance to Trondheim Fjord and brought the trawler to within five miles of the *Tirpitz*. Then, as luck would have it, a storm came up. The torpedoes broke loose from their towlines and sank before the frogmen could push them to their target.

In March of 1943, the *Tirpitz* moved to Alta Fjord. The following September, British reconnaissance planes, scouting across Norway between Murmansk and Scotland, spied the *Tirpitz* in its new lair and brought back detailed photographs, setting in motion another unorthodox plan.

The distance from Scotland to Alta Fjord and back, or even to Alta Fjord and on to a Russian airfield, was too far for British bombers. The next assault on the *Tirpitz* would have to come from the sea. The instruments

of attack were six midget submarines known as X-craft. Each was forty-eight-feet long, less than six feet in diameter, and carried a crew of four. Six regular submarines towed the midgets the 1,000 miles from Scotland to northern Norway. Off Alta Fjord, fresh crews replaced the old. Their mission was to approach the *Tirpitz* and the *Scharnhorst* undetected and plant mines under their bottoms.

Two of the X-craft were lost on the long voyage north. A third broke down at sea and had to be scuttled. During the approach to Alta Fjord, another mysteriously disappeared. The two remaining boats, the X-6 and the X-7, would limit their attack to the *Tirpitz*. In the early morning hours of September 22, after slipping through the outer torpedo nets guarding the *Tirpitz*'s anchorage, Lieutenant Donald Cameron, commanding the X-6, found a gap in the inner nets close to the battleship. Cameron barely had time to bless his luck when his little craft struck a sandbank. The X-6 bounced toward the surface, and a sailor on the *Tirpitz* spotted its periscope. The cry "Submarine!" went up, and at first incredulous seamen could only gawk at the sight as the X-6 resubmerged. That could have been the end of the midget submarine, which was only fifty yards from the towering battleship. But the *Tirpitz*'s guns could not be brought to bear on a target so close. Instead, the German sailors ran to fetch rifles and pistols.

The 50,000-ton *Tirpitz*, its deck camouflaged with evergreens, lies at anchor close to the treelined shore of Foettenfjord, near Trondheim, Norway. A crippling fuel shortage, lack of air support, and Hitler's fear of losing a capital ship kept the giant battleship in port for almost the entire war.

A visiting dance troupe entertains beneath the muzzles of the *Tirpitz*'s fifteen-inch guns. Such diversions, along with occasional hikes in the spectacular Norwegian countryside, helped the battleship's crew deal with a persistent enemy, boredom.

A few of them threw hand grenades toward the submarine's position, but they fell short. Meanwhile, Cameron and his crew came closer still and placed their charges before bobbing to the surface again.

A quick-thinking German officer hustled down the gangway to the *Tirpitz*'s launch, which was tied alongside, pushing some seamen ahead of him. Once near the surfaced submarine, he threw a line around its conning tower and tried hauling it away from the *Tirpitz*. At that point,

the hatch of the X-6 opened, and four oil-smeared men climbed out and surrendered. A minute or two later, the second submarine surfaced, just long enough to have the water around it churned to foam by small-arms fire from an aroused ship's company. It submerged again before any damage was done. The boat was the X-7, commanded by Lieutenant B. C. G. Place. After planting explosive charges under the *Tirpitz*'s hull, Place had been trying unsuccessfully to make a getaway.

Captain Hans Meyer, the battle-ship's commanding officer, sent divers to check the ship's underside. Meyer considered taking the *Tirpitz* into deeper water, but the presence of the X-7 changed his mind. Other submarines might be waiting there to torpedo him. He decided to warp the huge ship around by its anchor lines in case mines had been laid on the bottom of the fjord.

Lieutenant Cameron and the crew of the X-6, meanwhile, were brought aboard the *Tirpitz*, warmed with hot coffee and schnapps, and questioned. They could not resist glancing occasionally at their watches, but otherwise they communicated no useful information. The seconds ticked by. Suddenly, two explosions

The British submarine *Thrasher* tows an X-craft submarine out of Scotland's Loch Cairnbawn in September 1943. Two of the forty-one-foot-long midgets slipped into Kaafjord, Norway, and planted eight tons of mines that badly damaged the *Tirpitz*.

A Royal Air Force reconnaissance photo reveals the *Tirpitz* in its berth at Kaafjord, protected by torpedo nets. Between 1940 and 1944, British land- and sea-based bombers attacked the *Tirpitz* nineteen times.

rumbled through the ship. The *Tirpitz* shivered in place and the lights went out. Sailors were flung to the deck. Fire extinguishers fell off their bulkhead fittings and spewed chemicals along the passageways. Meanwhile, the X-7, which Lieutenant Place fully expected to be destroyed when the charges it had set went off, had become entangled in a torpedo net. The force of the blasts freed the submarine, and it popped again to the surface. Place and one crewman escaped before the damaged X-7 sank. The other two were not so fortunate.

The *Tirpitz* was still afloat. All four of its fifteen-inch-gun turrets had jumped their mounts, however, and one of the 5.9-inch guns was irreparably jammed. Fire-control mechanisms had been knocked awry. The port turbine casing, along with much of the rest of the engine machinery, had been cracked or bent. The ship's propellers could not turn, and flooding in the steering gear compartment made the port rudder unusable. Although the *Tirpitz*'s watertight integrity held, some small holes had been blown in its hull, and a number of hull frames were damaged. The other wounds could be fixed, but the damage to the frames could not. The *Tirpitz* was seriously crippled. Not until after the war would the British learn how effective the raid of the X-craft had been. For now, they still considered the battleship a major threat.

Skilled workmen performed repairs on the *Tirpitz* in Kaafjord, a deep-water cleft off Alta Fjord bounded by sheer walls of rock dotted with firs. Antiaircraft guns stood sentinel high on the cliffs. Torpedo nets again were

British airmen steady a Tallboy, the bomb that ultimately doomed the *Tirpitz*. The Tallboy was twenty-one feet long, weighed six tons, and carried enough high explosives to blow a hole in the ground eighty feet deep.

folded around the big ship, and a pipeline, capable of engulfing the entire fjord in a blanket of smoke in eight minutes, was laid around the walls of the inlet. During the months that followed, the British attacked the repair site several times by air, but their bombs exploded harmlessly nearby. On the night of February 11, 1944, the Russians tried their hand, dispatching fifteen heavy bombers, each carrying a single 2,000-pound bomb, from an air base near Archangel, 600 miles away. Despite good visibility, eleven of the planes failed to find the fjord, and the others missed the target.

Next came a series of raids by carrier-based Fairey Barracudas, dive bombers of the Royal Navy's air arm. Often the Germans were forewarned, and the Barracudas arrived to find the fjord hidden in manmade smoke, dotted here and there with darker puffs from the antiaircraft guns. Occasionally the pilots glimpsed the tip of the battleship's mast poking eerily through the gray. The flak was always intense, and at times the Barracudas came in so low that the guns on the cliffs actually fired down at them. One raid produced fifteen hits on the *Tirpitz* with bombs that weighed as much as 1,000 pounds. A few exploded on the armored turrets without effect. Some penetrated the upper deck, damaging several compartments and

Listening for sounds of life, German rescuers pace the upturned keel of the *Tirpitz* after the fateful British bombing raid of November 12, 1944. The boarding party saved the lives of eighty-five trapped crewmen by cutting holes in the hull with acetylene torches.

killing 122 sailors. But even this heavy bombardment failed to burst through the battleship's heaviest armor.

In mid-September of 1944, the frustrating task of destroying the *Tirpitz* was turned over to the RAF's Squadron 617, a team of experienced dambusters who flew Avro Lancasters and had been working to perfect the delivery of a new 12,000-pound bomb called the Tallboy. Unlike standard, tear-shaped bombs, the Tallboy had a sharply pointed nose made of casehardened steel. It was twenty-one feet long.

The distance from Scotland to Alta Fjord was still too far, even for long-range Lancasters. Their first strike, on September 15, was made with planes shuttled earlier to the Soviet Union. They reached the target—only after the fjord was full of smoke—dropped their bombs, and fled, thinking they had missed. Indeed, no Tallboy exploded inside the *Tirpitz*. But one of them pierced the deck at the battleship's graceful, overshot bow, sliced through the steel side plating, and exploded in the water. Its passage took it through the brig, where it killed one seaman, and the subsequent explosion folded back the foredeck like a sardine tin.

Admiral Dönitz decided that the *Tirpitz* could not be repaired on the scene or brought to the Reich's shipyards on the Baltic. Instead, he had it moved south to Tromso Sound to be used as a floating battery. If the *Tirpitz* were to be sunk, he wanted it to happen in shallow water where the ship would not turn over, no matter how hard it was hit. In theory, at least, its hull could rest on the fjord's bottom, and its guns could still cover the Norwegian coastline. So the *Tirpitz* dropped anchor near shore, over a shallow, sandy bottom, and dredges pushed sand up around its 850-foot-long hull.

Tromso Sound was 200 miles closer than Alta Fjord to the RAF bases in Scotland. When the *Tirpitz* was moved, British reconnaissance planes searched for it frantically, and this time they located it within forty-eight hours. The Lancaster bombers, meanwhile, had been fitted with new Rolls Royce engines. To reduce weight and make room for extra fuel, the planes were stripped of machine gun turrets and armor. The round trip to Tromso Sound required a range of nearly 2,000 miles. Without armor and shriven of half their guns, the Lancasters would be easy prey for German fighters flying out of Bardufoss, only a few miles from the *Tirpitz*'s new anchorage. With a two-ton overload of gas and bombs, the British reckoned that the Lancasters could just make it to the target and back.

Twenty-nine bombers flew from Scotland on November 12, 1944. Events conspired to make the raid a success. Warned of the attack, the *Tirpitz* called for fighter cover. None came. The Lancasters, cruising at 14,000 feet so that their accelerating bombs would pierce the *Tirpitz*'s armor before

During the winter and spring of 1945, the German navy, using every ship it could muster, carried off one of the largest seaborne rescues in history. The fleet shuttled back and forth across the Baltic Sea, between imperiled ports on the Gulf of Danzig and at Libau, in Lithuania, and relatively safe haven at Kiel and Copenhagen. Despite the menace of Soviet submarines, RAF bombers, and magnetic mines that had been dropped into the sea, the Germans evacuated more than two million soldiers and civilians a step ahead of the advancing Red Army.

exploding, met no airborne opposition, although the flak was heavy at first. The smoke-making machines on the ship were not yet operative, and those on shore were not as effective as they had been in the narrower waters of Kaafjord. For a change, the RAF bombardiers had a clear view of their target. The Tallboys fell silently away, and a series of thunderous explosions was followed by billowing columns of smoke. Three bombs had struck home, piercing the armored deck amidships, destroying two boilers and one engine room, and ripping a hole forty-five feet long in the hull's port side from the bilge keel to the upper deck. Fires raging through the ship ignited a magazine, and the *Tirpitz* was racked by a deafening explosion. As they banked for home, the crew of the last Lancaster caught a glimpse of the ship's red bottom. It was capsizing after all.

The jolting explosions destroyed all means of communication within the *Tirpitz*. The men deep in the windowless communications center did not realize at first that their ship was slowly turning over. They were duty bound not to leave their stations, but when the deck began to slant dras-

A Perilous Shuttle to Safety

Fleeing the Red Army, German civilians leave their wagons behind and walk across the treacherous sea ice to reach evacuation ships in the Frisches Haff, a twelve-mile-wide lagoon separating the East Prussian mainland from the Baltic Sea.

tically, they hurried to reach topside. Several others joined them, climbing ladders at bizarre angles, backtracking as their way was blocked by fallen equipment. The ship kept turning. Trying to smash open a jammed hatch, the trapped men realized that they were scrambling along the slanted overhead. Then they heard the ominous rush of water. They were still several decks from what should have been escape, except that the *Tirpitz* was now upside down.

Fighting panic, the crewmen realized that in the shallow anchorage the bottom of the ship's hull should be above water. Pursued by inrushing water, they scrambled back the way they had come. At one point, they were joined by a stoker who, along with dozens of rats, had squirmed out of an engine room through a tube that carried electric cables. Finally, they heard footsteps above them. Potential rescuers were tramping around on the dead ship's bottom. A seaman banged on the hull in Morse code: "Sixteen men under oil tank forward workshop."

German sailors chop ice from the deck of their ship in preparation for taking on refugees. Warships offshore provided covering fire to protect the refugee-laden vessels from enemy attack.

Great crashing noises followed—the sound of pieces of the outer hull, cut by acetylene torches, smashing against the inner hull. When the inner hull, too, had been cut, the pressure of escaping air roared through the openings, extinguishing the torches and interrupting the rescue. It was Sunday morning, and the ship's senior engineer officer had been ashore attending a church service when the attack occurred. After commandeering every acetylene torch in Tromso, he organized rescue teams and showed them where to cut.

The operation went on all day and night. By late Sunday afternoon, the first men were brought out. The last to get out alive were freed after almost twenty-four hours. In all, the cutting produced eighty-five survivors. Many of the others drowned, the water rising around them even as their mates above tried frantically to slice through in time. The men standing on the ship's keel listened in horror to the muffled farewells of the doomed sailors and heard them singing the national anthem, "Deutschland, Deutschland

über Alles." Of a crew of about 1,800, nearly 1,000 were dead or missing, many of them entombed in the vessel that must have seemed invincible.

After the death of the *Tirpitz*, the saga of the German surface fleet entered a final chapter that coincided with the last months of the Third Reich. Perhaps fittingly, the drama was played out in the Baltic Sea, an arm of the Atlantic enclosed by Denmark and the Scandinavian Peninsula. More than 900 miles long and no more than 100 miles wide along most of its length, the Baltic is a shallow, sandy-bottomed body of water given to nasty storms and high, choppy waves. For nearly four years, the Baltic had been a German lake, and here, through the winter and spring of 1945, the men and ships of the beleaguered Kriegsmarine enjoyed their finest hour.

During the autumn of 1944, the Red Army, 225 divisions strong, drove across the Vistula River into Poland, threatening to cut off East Prussia as well as Estonia, Lithuania, and Latvia. For a brief period, the forty undermanned divisions of Germany's Army Group North had a chance to fall back and keep open a line of retreat. But Hitler issued a series of directives ordering his army to "fight where you stand," and the opportunity was lost.

The day came when the cruiser *Emden*, the first big ship built for the modern German navy, was ordered to Königsberg for refit. The cruiser's captain then received instructions to stand by to sail on short notice. As the crew waited, a heavy snowfall muffled the sound of Soviet artillery thudding in the distance. At three o'clock on the morning of January 24, two trucks with a uniformed guard came down the quay and unloaded two large caskets. The *Emden*'s cargo was to be the remains of Field Marshal Paul von Hindenburg and his wife, Gertrud, disinterred from the mausoleum at Tannenberg, some seventy miles inland, to prevent them from falling into Russian hands. The aristocratic World War I hero and president of the Weimar Republic had appointed Hitler chancellor in 1933. Hindenburg's son Oskar boarded the ship that night as well. He did not know where the caskets of his parents would come to rest, or even if he would live to bury them again, and he wanted a moment to say good-bye.

By January of 1945, the Russian juggernaut had cut northward to the Baltic. The only escape route remaining was the sea. From Memel on the Lithuanian coast, south past Königsberg, and along the Bay of Danzig, beachheads had to be held at all costs. It was at these last, desperate footholds, shielding a German army with its back to the sea, that the surface fleet finally showed its full mettle. In the spring of 1945, German ships would fire more shells than they had in the previous five years of war.

For weeks, the *Scheer* and the *Prinz Eugen*, abetted by the *Lützow*, the dusted-off *Hipper*, the cruisers *Köln* and *Emden*, and the old battleships

In the wake of an RAF attack, the passenger liner *Cap Arcona* *(foreground)* lies on its side in the shallows of Neustadt harbor near the burned-out steamer *Deutschland*. Most of the 5,000 prisoners held on the *Cap Arcona* were trapped on the lower decks or drowned after abandoning ship.

A victim of the bombing washes up amid flotsam from the *Cap Arcona*. Many of the emaciated concentration camp inmates who leaped overboard could not cope with the forty-five-degree water and succumbed to hypothermia.

Supervised by British soldiers, residents of Neustadt dig a mass grave on the beach for casualties of the bombing. Before burial, bodies still wearing prison garb were identified by the numbers on their uniforms.

A Prison Ship Bombed by Mistake

A tragic mistake scarred the sealift that carried German soldiers and civilian refugees to safety in the war's chaotic final days. As the Allies swept closer, the inmates of Neuengamme concentration camp—10,000 men and boys from half a dozen nations—were transferred by the SS to ships of the evacuation fleet anchored at the Baltic port of Neustadt.

On the afternoon of May 3, 1945, a squadron of single-engine Typhoon fighter-bombers appeared over Neustadt. The RAF pilots had orders to stop German troops and high-ranking Nazis from leaving port, and they launched rockets armed with new sixty-five-pound incendiary warheads at the prison ships. Forty of the rockets hit the *Cap Arcona*, the prewar pride of the Hamburg-Südamerika steamship company, and turned the perilously overcrowded liner into a flaming pyre. Other rockets set the nearby freighter *Thielbek* and the steamship *Deutschland* aflame.

The ships were close to shore, but they burned and sank so fast that most of their human cargo never had a chance. Eight thousand captives and crew members died. Later that day, troops of the British army marched into Neustadt and accepted the city's surrender.

Schleswig-Holstein and *Schlesien*, trained their guns on the advancing Russians. The *Scheer* did such deadly work that grateful German soldiers came aboard just to shake hands with the crew. Off Riga and elsewhere, the *Prinz Eugen's* gunners had a Luftwaffe spotter plane and army forward observers finding targets for them. Working together, as they seldom had before, they wreaked havoc on Soviet tank columns and artillery units.

Every ship kept firing until its ammunition ran out. Then it steamed back to Kiel or Swinemünde for more. The guns were so hard-used that their barrel linings wore out and had to be replaced. The massive offshore firepower helped buy several months of reprieve for the collapsing Reich and enabled millions of soldiers and civilians to escape to the West. The refugees began to come in the dead of winter, some riding in farm carts and sleighs, but most of them on foot. Wave upon wave of them poured into Memel and Königsberg, the capital of East Prussia, and squeezed past the city to its port of Pillau.

A pair of long, narrow sandspits, the Hela Peninsula and the Frische Nehrung, jut from the Polish mainland into the Bay of Danzig. By spring, almost every square yard of these narrow peninsulas was crowded with

On October 15, 1944, the often-battered heavy cruiser *Prinz Eugen* collided with the light cruiser *Leipzig* in the Bay of Danzig, striking the smaller ship broadside with its sharp bow. In the sequence below, damage-control teams make emergency repairs to prevent the *Leipzig* from sinking *(left)*; after several hours, the *Prinz Eugen* pulls free *(center)*, revealing a deep gouge *(right)* that extended all the way to the *Leipzig's* keel. The ship was permanently damaged.

refugees. For every thousand taken off by a motley rescue fleet, thousands more arrived. The Red Army shelled the beaches. Each night, the refugees slapped together flimsy docks and used them to board the small craft that ferried them out to the larger vessels that were to take them to safety. Each day, Soviet aircraft shot them to pieces.

Dönitz put Rear Admiral Konrad Engelhardt in charge of all rescue operations. By Dönitz's order, "every ship, every cruiser, destroyer, torpedo boat, merchant ship, fishing boat, and rowboat" was pressed into service. The result was history's biggest and most successful seaborne evacuation. Between late January and early May of 1945, nearly 550,000 soldiers and perhaps as many as two million civilians were evacuated.

When the ice melted in the Gulf of Finland, Soviet submarines came south to lie in ambush along the escape route to Kiel. The RAF appeared in greater numbers, bombing the ports and dropping magnetic mines in the sea lanes. Inevitably, some of the ships that pulled out of Memel and Pillau and Hela, their decks thick with refugees, met tragic ends. On the night of January 30, the overloaded passenger ship *Wilhelm Gustloff* was torpedoed and four thousand people drowned—twice as many as died on

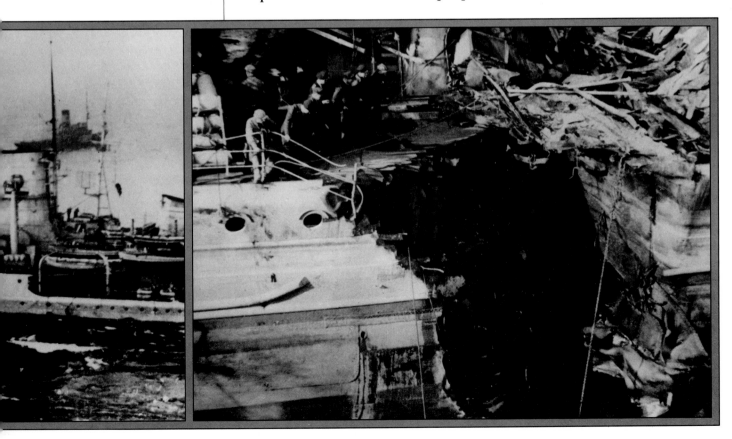

On May 7, 1945, the crews of German torpedo boats form up in Geltinger Bay, near the Danish border, to haul down their swastika ensigns for the last time.

the *Titanic* and the *Lusitania* combined. On February 10, the *General von Steuben* was sunk, along with all but 300 of its 3,400 passengers and crew. In April, 6,830 more deaths occurred when the transport *Goya* was sunk. Still, losses at sea were less than two percent of the number of people saved.

The surviving ships of the German navy shuttled back and forth to the embattled ports. They fired salvos over the heads of retreating soldiers at the oncoming Russians and ran in tons of food, ammunition, and coal to the shrinking bridgeheads. Not a single big ship was hit at sea, but the RAF took its toll in the harbors. In December, the venerable *Schleswig-Holstein* succumbed to bombs and settled on an even keel in Gotenhafen on the Gulf of Danzig. The crew stubbornly manned their guns for another month before abandoning ship. On April 9, the *Admiral Scheer* was sunk at Kiel. The *Lützow* was badly damaged at Swinemünde on April 16 and, like the *Schleswig-Holstein*, served as a gun platform until the Germans blew it up to keep it from falling to the Allies.

Only the *Prinz Eugen* remained lucky, as it had been on a pitch-black night in the fall of 1944 when it sliced into the *Leipzig* amidships, almost cutting the smaller ship in two. The *Prinz Eugen* dared not back away for fear the *Leipzig* would flood. For fourteen hours, the two ships drifted, locked together, until tugboats arrrived to help separate them. The *Leipzig* was never the same again, but after two weeks in the yard, the *Prinz Eugen* was as good as new.

At both ends of the Baltic, the bombing grew more furious. The perimeters of land still in German hands shrank to a few square miles. On April 30, 1945, Hitler killed himself in his bunker as Soviet troops ransacked Berlin. He had appointed Dönitz to succeed him. Practical as always, the grand admiral negotiated with the French, Americans, and British for a temporary cease-fire in the west, hoping to gain a few extra days to save additional troops and refugees from the Russians. General Dwight D. Eisenhower, supreme commander of the Allied forces, would accept nothing less than unconditional surrender on all fronts, and during three days of talks, the bloodletting continued.

Seeing he could do no more, Dönitz ordered his naval commanders to turn over their vessels when the surrender went into effect at 1:00 a.m. on May 9. Although most complied, unofficial boatlifts continued for several days. Of the major ships of the High Seas Fleet, only two crippled cruisers, the *Leipzig* and the *Nürnberg*, remained. And, of course, the *Prinz Eugen*. After the war, the *Prinz* was destined to be assaulted again, as part of the 1946 atomic bomb tests near Bikini in the Pacific Ocean. It was one of the few sacrificial ships in the test that refused to sink. A year later, the indestructible cruiser was broken up for scrap. ✠

Gallant Missions of Mercy

The German navy's final mission in 1945 was to evacuate the soldiers and civilians fleeing East Prussia ahead of the oncoming Red Army. This ultimate test of discipline and nerve became the navy's finest hour. The high command organized a thousand ships, many of them unused for years and barely seaworthy, and staffed them with whatever military and merchant mariners could be found. In some cases, officers lacking in experience or resolve were replaced by men accustomed to improvising under trying conditions.

Some ships traveled from Danish and north German ports to East Prussia ten or more times, delivering supplies to beleaguered troops and returning crammed with refugees and wounded. As fuel grew scarce and attrition took its toll, the burden shifted from passenger liners, freighters, and warships to smaller craft. Working through the war's final hours, they brought out more than two million refugees.

A boat breaking a channel in the ice *(right foreground)* moves through the congested harbor at Pillau in late January 1945. The East Prussian port teemed with refugees *(inset)*, who crowded onto rescue ships with their meager belongings.

A motley evacuation fleet, including a passenger steamer *(right)* and many smaller vessels, takes advantage of a break in the weather to run for the relative safety of Danish and German Baltic ports. Passengers overflowed onto the decks and into the lifeboats of the larger transports *(far left)*, and those on smaller boats made the entire voyage in the open *(left)*.

Left behind, a goat stands tethered to an abandoned wagon on the quay at Pillau. Refugees might leave home with many possessions, but they were allowed to embark with only what they could carry. Although some ships, like the two shown here, carried antiaircraft guns, they usually sailed at night to reduce the chance of attack.

Soldiers on the training ship *Hektor* watch rescue boats take passengers off the aged battleship *Schlesien*, which is down at the stern and sinking after hitting a mine near Swinemünde on May 3. On the following day, bombers sank the *Hektor*, which earlier had fought as the sea raider *Orion*. Other troops were lost on shore: Almost 4,000 men of the Gross-deutschland Division reached Pillau *(inset)*, but only 800 of them escaped the port.

On a dock in Copenhagen in early May, exhausted refugees wait in the warming sun for word that Germany has surrendered. Behind them, riding high for lack of fuel and ammunition but still intact after five years of war, is the heavy cruiser *Prinz Eugen*.

Acknowledgments

The editors thank the following individuals and institutions for their help: England: London—Terry Charman, Paul Kemp, Allan Williams, Mike Willis, Imperial War Museum. Federal Republic of Germany: Berlin—Heidi Klein, Bildarchiv Preussischer Kulturbesitz; Wolfgang Streubel, Ullstein Bilderdienst. Cuxhaven—Horst Bredow, U-Boot-Archiv. Flensburg—Magdalena Kossack, Eberhard Schmidt, Marineschule Mürwik. Freiburg—Hansjoseph Maierhöfer, Bundesarchiv/Militärarchiv. Harmsdorf—Jochen Brennecke. Herrsching—Burkard Freiherr von Müllenheim-Rechberg. Koblenz—Meinrad Nilges, Bundesarchiv. Munich—Elisabeth Heidt, Süddeutscher Verlag Bilderdienst; Kapitän-zur-See Otto Koehler. Neustadt—Wilhelm Lange, Stadtarchiv. Seevetal—Günther Schwarberg. Wasbek—Hermann Lindner. United States: District of Columbia—Defense Mapping Agency; Elizabeth Hill, Jim Trimble, National Archives; Tamara Moser Melia, Naval Historical Center; Eveline Nave, Library of Congress; George Snowden, Snowden Associates. Maryland—Mary Beth Straight, U.S. Naval Institute. New Jersey—Al Collett. South Carolina—Lyal Stryker, Association of Minemen. Virginia—George A. Petersen, National Capital Historical Sales.

Picture Credits

Credits from left to right are separated by semicolons, from top to bottom by dashes. Cover: Imperial War Museum, London. 4: Bundesarchiv, Koblenz. 6: Bildarchiv Preussischer Kulturbesitz, West Berlin. 8, 9: Camera Press, London. 10: Ullstein Bilderdienst, West Berlin. 11: Bildarchiv Preussischer Kulturbesitz, West Berlin—from *Erich Raeder: Mein Leben* (Vol. 1), Schlichtenmayer, Tübingen, 1956, courtesy Marineschule Mürwik. 15: National Archives, no. 306-NT-1290B-29. 16: National Archives, no. 242-HB-20475-1—National Archives, no. 242-HB-20475-7. 18, 19: Robert Hunt Library, London. 20: Bayerisches Hauptstaatsarchiv, Munich—from *Hitler und die bildende Künste* by Klaus Backes, Dumont Buchverlag, Köln, 1988. 23: UPI/Bettmann Newsphotos, New York. 24, 25: UPI/Bettmann Newsphotos (2)—Globe Photos, New York. 26, 27: S.I.R.P.A./E.C.P. Armées, Paris. 31: Popperfoto, London. 32, 33: From *The Battle of the River Plate* by Dudley Pope, William Kimber and Co., London, 1956; Topham Picture Source, Edenbridge. 34, 35: Robert Hunt Library, London. 36, 37: Süddeutscher Verlag Bilderdienst, Munich; Wide World Photos, New York—U.S. Navy. 38, 39: Painting by Attila Heija. 40-43: Artwork by John Batchelor, copied by Larry Sherer. 44: U.S. Navy. 46, 47: Maps by R. R. Donnelley and Sons Company, Cartographic Services. 51: Bundesarchiv, Koblenz. 52: Süddeutscher Verlag Bilderdienst, Munich—artwork by William J. Hennessy, Jr. 54, 55: U.S. Naval Institute. 56: U.S. Navy. 59: Norsk Telegrambyrå, Oslo—Süddeutscher Verlag Bilderdienst, Munich. 60, 61: Norsk Telegrambyrå, Oslo. 63: Süddeutscher Verlag Bilderdienst, Munich. 64, 65: Ullstein Bilderdienst, West Berlin. 67: From *Das grosse Bildbuch der Deutschen Kriegsmarine 1939-1945* by Cajus Bekker, Gerhard Stalling Verlag, Oldenburg, 1972, courtesy Lis Berenbrok. 69: WZ-Bilderdienst, Wilhelmshaven. 70, 71: WZ-Bilderdienst, Wilhelmshaven, except lower left Bundesarchiv, Koblenz. 75: Hulton Picture Company, London. 76: Bundesarchiv, Koblenz. 78, 79: Hilfs-Kreuzer Pinguin-Stamm, Kiel (2)—map by R. R. Donnelley and Sons Company, Cartographic Services. 80, 81: Hilfs-Kreuzer Pinguin-Stamm, Kiel. 82, 83: Hilfs-Kreuzer Pinguin-Stamm, Kiel, except lower right from *Cruise of the Raider HK-33* by H. J. Brennecke, Thomas Y. Crowell Co., New York, 1955. 84, 85: Bundesarchiv, Koblenz, except upper left, Hilfs-Kreuzer Pinguin-Stamm, Kiel. 86, 87: From *Ghost Cruiser H.K. 33* by H. J. Brennecke, William Kimber and Co., London, 1955. 88, 89: Hilfs-Kreuzer Pinguin-Stamm, Kiel—Bundesarchiv, Koblenz (2). 90-93: Hilfs-Kreuzer Pinguin-Stamm, Kiel. 94: From *Kreuzer Prinz Eugen...unter 3 Flaggen* by Paul Schmalenbach, Koehlers Verlagsgesellschaft, Herford, 1978. 96: Archives Tallandier, Paris. 99: Bundesarchiv, Koblenz. 100, 101: Official U.S. Navy photograph. 102, 103: Bildarchiv Preussischer Kulturbesitz, West Berlin. 105: Robert Hunt Library, London (2)—from *Battleships: Axis and Neutral Battleships in World War II* by William H. Garzke, Jr., and Robert O. Dulin, Jr., Naval Institute Press, Annapolis, Md., 1985. 107: Map by R. R. Donnelley and Sons Company, Cartographic Services. 108, 109: Topham Picture Source, Edenbridge. 110, 111: Robert Hunt Library, London. 113: Larry Sherer, courtesy of the collection of Ed Owen. 115: From *German Raiders of World War II* by August Karl Muggenthaler, Prentice-Hall, Englewood Cliffs, N.J., 1977. 117: U.S. Navy. 118, 119: UPI/Bettmann Newsphotos; Bundesarchiv, Koblenz. 120, 121: From *The Rand McNally Encyclopedia of Military Aircraft 1914-1980*, Military Press, New York, 1983—Süddeutscher Verlag Bilderdienst, Munich. 123: Bundesarchiv, Koblenz—Danish Royal Library. 124, 125: Robert Hunt Library, London; U.S. Naval Institute. 126: U.S. Navy. 128: Bundesarchiv, Koblenz. 129: From *Kreuzer Prinz Eugen...unter 3 Flaggen* by Paul Schmalenbach, Koehlers Verlagsgesellschaft, Herford, 1978. 130-133: Bundesarchiv, Koblenz. 134: Robert Hunt Library, London—Bundesarchiv, Koblenz. 135: Bundesarchiv, Koblenz. 136, 137: Bundesarchiv, Koblenz; Robert Hunt Library, London. 138: U.S. Navy. 139: Imperial War Museum, London. 140, 141: Bundesarchiv, Koblenz. 142: From *Die versunkene Flotte: Deutsche Schlachtschiffe und Kreuzer 1925-45*, edited by Cajus Bekker, Gerhard Stalling Verlag, Oldenburg, 1961, courtesy of Lis Berenbrok. 144: U.S. Navy. 147: Map by R. R. Donnelley and Sons Company, Cartographic Services. 148, 149: Imperial War Museum, London. 150: Ullstein Bilderdienst, West Berlin. 154, 155: Robert Hunt Library, London. 158: U.S. Naval Institute, Annapolis, Md. 159: Robert Hunt Library, London. 160, 161: Submarine Museum, Gosport, Hants; from *The German Navy in World War II: A Reference Guide to the Kriegsmarine, 1935-45* by Jak P. Mallmann Showell, Naval Institute Press, Annapolis, Md., 1979, courtesy Imperial War Museum. 162, 163: From *The Death of the Tirpitz* by Ludovic Kennedy, Little, Brown and Company, Boston, 1979. 165: Map by R. R. Donnelley and Sons Company, Cartographic Services. 166: Süddeutscher Verlag Bilderdienst, Munich. 167: From *Flucht über die Ostsee 1944/45 im Bild* by Heinz Schön, Motorbuch Verlag Stuttgart, 1985. 169: WZ-Bilderdienst, Wilhelmshaven. 170, 171: From *Die Cap Arcona-Katastrophe* by Heinz Schön, Motorbuch Verlag Stuttgart, 1989 (2)—Archiv Günther Schwarberg, Seevetal. 172: Robert Hunt Library, London; Imperial War Museum, London (2). 174, 175: Imperial War Museum, London. 176, 177: Bundesarchiv, Koblenz. 178, 179: Bundesarchiv, Koblenz; Süddeutscher Verlag Bilderdienst, Munich—Imperial War Museum, London. 180, 181: Carl Henrich, Traben-Trarbach. 182, 183: Ullstein Bilderdienst, West Berlin, Wolfgang Hoheisel, inset GD-Bild-Archiv, Eching/Ammersee. 184, 185: Carl Henrich, Traben-Trarbach.

Bibliography

Books

Bartels, Hans, *Tigerflagge Heiss Vor!* Bielefeld, W.Ger.: Deutscher Heimatverlag Ernst Gieseking, 1943.

Bekker, Cajus:
Hitler's Naval War. Transl. and ed. by Frank Ziegler. Garden City, N.Y.: Doubleday, 1974.
Die versunkene Flotte. Oldenburg, W.Ger.: Gerhard Stalling Verlag, 1964.

Bekker, C. D., *Defeat at Sea.* New York: Henry Holt, 1955.

Brennecke, H. J., *Cruise of the Raider HK-33.* New York: Thomas Y. Crowell, 1954.

Brennecke, Jochen, *Schlachtschiff Tirpitz.* Hamm, W.Ger.: Deutscher See-Verlag, 1953.

Breyer, Siegfried, *Die Deutsche Kriegsmarine 1935-1945* (Vol. 2). Friedberg, W.Ger.: Podzun-Pallas Verlag, 1986.

Brown, David, *Tirpitz: The Floating Fortress.* Annapolis, Md.: Naval Institute Press, 1977.

Churchill, Winston S., *The Gathering Storm* (Vol. 1 of *The Second World War*). Boston: Houghton Mifflin, 1948.

Doenitz, Karl, *Memoirs: Ten Years and Twenty Days.* Transl. by R. H. Stevens. Cleveland: World Publishing, 1959.

Elting, John R., and the Editors of Time-Life Books, *Battles for Scandinavia* (World War II series). Alexandria, Va.: Time-Life Books, 1981.

Frank, Wolfgang, and Bernhard Rogge, *The German Raider Atlantis.* Transl. by R. O. B. Long. New York: Ballantine Books, 1956.

Frere-Cook, Gervis, *The Attacks on the Tirpitz.* Annapolis, Md.: Naval Institute Press, 1973.

Fuehrer Conferences on Naval Affairs 1939-1945. Annapolis, Md.: Naval Institute Press, 1990.

Garzke, William H., Jr., and Robert O. Dulin, Jr., *Battleships: Axis and Neutral Battleships in World War II.* Annapolis, Md.: Naval Institute Press, 1985.

Grube, Frank, and Gerhard Richter, *Flucht und Vertreibung.* Hamburg, W.Ger.: Hoffmann und Campe, 1981.

Humble, Richard, *Hitler's High Seas Fleet.*
New York: Ballantine Books, 1971.

Irving, David, *The Destruction of Convoy PQ.17.* New York: Simon and Schuster, 1968.

Jane's Fighting Ships of World War II. London: Bracken Books, 1989.

Kennedy, Ludovic:
The Death of the Tirpitz. Boston: Little, Brown, 1979.
Menace: The Life and Death of the Tirpitz. London: Sidgwick & Jackson, 1979.

Koburger, Charles W., Jr., *Steel Ships, Iron Crosses, and Refugees.* New York: Praeger, 1989.

Krancke, Theodor, and H. J. Brennecke, *The Battleship Scheer.* London: William Kimber, 1956.

Martienssen, Anthony, *Hitler and His Admirals.* New York: E. P. Dutton, 1949.

Muggenthaler, August Karl, *German Raiders of World War II.* Englewood Cliffs, N. J.: Prentice-Hall, 1977.

Müllenheim-Rechberg, Burkard von:
Battleship Bismarck: A Survivor's Story. Annapolis, Md.: Naval Institute Press, 1980.
Schlachtschiff Bismarck. Frankfurt/Main, W.Ger.: Verlag Ullstein, 1990.

Pope, Dudley, *The Battle of the River Plate.* London: Pan Books, 1974.

Powell, Michael, *Death in the South Atlantic: The Last Voyage of the Graf Spee.* New York: Rinehart, 1957.

Raeder, Erich:
My Life. Transl. by Henry W. Drexel. Annapolis, Md.: United States Naval Institute, 1960.
Struggle for the Sea. London: William Kimber, 1959.

Robertson, Terence, *Channel Dash.* London: Evans Brothers, 1958.

Rohwer, J., and G. Hummelchen, *Chronology of the War at Sea 1939-1945* (Vol. 1). Transl. by Derek Masters. London: Ian Allan, 1972.

Ruge, Friedrich, *Der Seekrieg.* Transl. by M. G. Saunders. Annapolis, Md.: United States Naval Institute, 1957.

Rutherford, Ward, *Hitler's Propaganda Machine.* London: Bison Books, 1985.

Schmalenbach, Paul, *Kreuzer Prinz Eugen . . . unter 3 Flaggen.* Herford, W.Ger.: Koehlers Verlagsgesellschaft, 1978.

Schofield, B. B., *The Russian Convoys.* Philadelphia: Dufour Editions, 1964.

Schön, Heinz:
Die Cap Arcona-Katastrophe. Stuttgart, W.Ger.: Motorbuch Verlag, 1989.
Flucht über die Ostsee. Stuttgart, W.Ger.: Motorbuch Verlag, 1985.

Showell, Jak P. Mallmann, *The German Navy in World War Two.* Annapolis, Md.: Naval Institute Press, 1979.

Van der Vat, Dan, *The Atlantic Campaign.* New York: Harper & Row, 1988.

Von der Porten, Edward P., *The German Navy in World War II.* New York: Thomas Y. Crowell, 1972.

Watts, A. J., *The Loss of the Scharnhorst.* London: Ian Allan, 1970.

Whitley, M. J.:
Destroyer! London: Arms and Armour Press, 1983.
German Cruisers of World War Two. Annapolis, Md.: Naval Institute Press, 1987.

Wingate, John, ed., *Warships in Profile* (Vol. 2). Garden City, N.Y.: Doubleday, 1973.

Woodward, David:
The Secret Raiders. New York: W. W. Norton, 1955.
The Tirpitz and the Battle for the North Atlantic. New York: W. W. Norton, 1954.

Other Publications

Ballard, Robert D., "Finding the *Bismarck*." *National Geographic*, November 1989.

Doenitz, Karl, "The Conduct of the War at Sea." Essay. Washington, D.C.: U.S. Department of the Navy, Division of Naval Intelligence, January 15, 1946.

"German Underwater Ordnance Mines." Bureau of Ordnance Publication OP 1673A. Great Lakes, Ill.: U.S. Department of the Navy, Electronics/Ordnance Department, June 14, 1946.

Schmalenbach, Paul S., and James E. Wise, Jr., "Pictorial—*Prinz Eugen* Album." *U. S. Naval Institute Proceedings* No. 8, Vol. 95, no. 798, Annapolis, Md., August 1969.

Index

Numerals in italics indicate an illustration of the subject mentioned.

Time-Life Books Inc. offers a wide range of fine recordings, including a *Rock 'n' Roll Era* series. For subscription information, call 1-800-621-7026 or write Time-Life Music, P.O. Box C-32068, Richmond, Virginia 23261-2068.